IMMORTAL FACES:

JULIA MARGARET CAMERON ON THE ISLE OF WIGHT

by Brian Hinton

"Genius and love have each fulfilled their part,
and both unite with force and equal grace,
whilst all that we love best in classic art
is stamped forever on the immortal face".

Julia Margaret Cameron, "On a Portrait", September 1875

"I longed to arrest all beauty that came before me, and at length the longing has been satisfied. Its difficulty enhanced the value of the pursuit. The peasantry of our Island is very handsome. From the men, the women, the maidens and the children I have had very lovely subjects, as all the patrons of my photography know".

Julia Margaret Cameron, "Annals of My Glass House" 1874

To the memory of Richard J. Hutchings

Acknowledgements

The following includes, in as far as possible, only facts that can be checked against written evidence or indisputable witness, I myself bear witness to the late Richard Hutchings, and to Joy Lester, Charles Everest, Mary Clark, Dr Jack Jones, Don Kennett, John Smart, Roy Toms and others who have provided local information.

I am indebted to Colin Ford; to Amanda Hopkinson for permission to quote from her book 'Julia Margaret Cameron'; and to Michael Mattis and Judy Hochberg of Los Alamos, New Mexico.

Eric Toogood, Johanna Jones, Dick Orchard, Mrs Butler and Clifford Webster have kindly provided corrections to work in progress. I am particularly grateful to Heather Freeman, who has reshaped random thoughts into a coherent whole.

Any inaccuracies I take as my own.

Brian Hinton

First Edition 1992, reprinted 2001

ISBN 1 870947 13 4

Jointly published by Isle of Wight County Press Ltd. and
Isle of Wight County Council

Printed by Isle of Wight County Press Ltd.
Brannon House, Pyle Street, Newport, Isle of Wight

Contents

Foreword

Immortal Faces further documents the work of Julia Margaret Cameron, the celebrated 19th century photographer who lived and did most of her outstanding work here on the Isle of Wight.

The book itself was conceived by the librarian at Freshwater Public Library — Dr. Brian Hinton, M.A. (Oxon), PhD — whose knowledge of Julia Margaret Cameron, Alfred Lord Tennyson and the other notable Victorians who lived in or visited the Isle of Wight is unmatched here.

Thanks are due to artist and fellow Councillor Charles Chapman, my Vice-Chairman, for his support in enabling this book to receive the backing of the County Council.

Thanks are also due to Morris Barton, Leader of the County Council, for finding the necessary share of the finance required to enable a joint publication to go ahead with the Isle of Wight County Press. The managing director of that newspaper, Robin Freeman, is to be thanked for offering, in these hard times, to co-operate in this worthwhile work. Credit is due to Royston Futter — a former employee of the Isle of Wight Cultural Services Department — for realizing, many years ago, the value of Cameron's album and ensuring its proper conservation and safety.

In Julia Margaret Cameron, the Island has a jewel in its crown. Due to the efforts of local conservationist Richard Greenwood, a Preservation Trust has been formed to save her former home Dimbola Lodge (now Dimbola and Cameron House) from demolition. The Trust can be contacted through the Cultural Services Department of the Isle of Wight County Council, and every assistance will be given to all who are interested in preserving and furthering the knowledge and understanding of Cameron's work.

If there is anyone I have neglected to acknowledge, please forgive me.

Ron Smith, C.C.
Chairman, Isle of Wight County Council's
Amenities & Countryside Committee 1992

Preface

Julia Margaret Cameron lived the sort of life in which she need never make a bed nor boil an egg. Yet she took up photography in an era when it could not have been more cumbersome, complex or dangerous. She had to make/mix her own chemicals (including gun cotton, a volatile explosive); spread them evenly on a large sheet of spotlessly clean glass; and take a picture before the photo-sensitive formula had dried out.

The likelihood of such an eccentric, wayward and untidy woman overcoming these technical difficulties to create some of the greatest portraits of the nineteenth century — in any medium — seems remote. Yet, miraculously, that is exactly what she did, as the 'immortal faces' in this book prove.

Mrs. Cameron's first camera took 11 in. x 9 in. (28 cm x 23 cm) negatives; later, she increased the size to 15 in. x 12 in. (38 cm x 30 cm). Thus, she was perhaps the first to take 'Life-sized heads' (*see* page 64). The startling effect of these early 'close-ups' on Victorians, used to tiny *carte de visite* portraits (a mere 4 in. x 2¼ in. (10 x 5.7 cm), is difficult to imagine.

In time, Julia Margaret decided to emulate the immensely popular *cartes:* all the pictures in this book are in this format. Unlike those of the professionals, hers were not taken specially, but reduced from her large originals (*see* page 37). Unlike others, too, they were presented with a fine gold line framing the picture. This set them apart from run-of-the-mill miniature photographs, just as the quality of Mrs Cameron's photographs lifts them head and shoulders above any of her contemporaries.

The house where Julia Margaret Cameron took up photography, and where the majority of her masterpieces were taken, still stands; a rare, perhaps unique, survival. Its demolition would be a tragedy.

Colin Ford
Head, National Museum of Photography, Film & Television

Julia Cameron: A Brief Biography

Early Life

Julia Margaret Cameron, recently described as"the greatest pictorial photographer of the 19th century", was a daughter of the Raj, born in Calcutta on Sunday June 11th 1815.

She was one of that extraordinary family the Pattles, descended through her mother, Adeline de l'Etang, from a French family of the ancien regime, who fled Paris after the revolution. Adeline's father, the Chevalier Ambrose de L'Etang, had been a page of honour to Marie Antoinette, to whom he had shown great devotion; a devotion so great that he was exiled to India and thus, literally, kept his head.

It is thus no coincidence that Mrs Cameron's central role in the Freshwater of the 1860s was both as photographer and society hostess. In the words of Wilfred Ward, the artistic colony there

"approached nearer to realizing the purpose and ideal of a French salon than any social group I have myself known in England. It is, of course, startling to compare people who met in the most informal way in the green lanes of the Isle of Wight, and at the houses of friends who were for the most part in no sense people of fashion, with such Parisian a coterie as was grouped around Madame Récamier and Chateaubriand.

Nevertheless, it appears to me that the ideal of the salon, which has proved so impossible to realise in London, was largely realised in Freshwater. We had our Chateaubriand in Tennyson, and, surprising as the comparison may be, we had our Madame Récamier in Mrs Cameron. The essential work of gathering together the interesting people who were to form the Tennyson society, the enthusiasm for the hero and for genius in general, was Mrs Cameron's part, as it was Madame Récamier's."

Julia was the fourth born of a family of ten children. Seven, all girls, survived into adulthood, and were to enliven the Victorian cultural scene.

As Hester Thackeray Fuller relates,

"Before her marriage she was one of the well known Miss Pattles, one of whom became Mrs Prinsep and was celebrated for her salon at Little Holland House; another, Countess Somers, who was renowned for her beauty; another, Lady Dalrymple, who was beloved for her kindness, each one of the seven sisters being remarkable in a different way"

It was said that Raj society divided into *"men, women and Pattles"*, a name which became synonymous with oddity and a flouting of Victorian conventions.

Julia's father was a Scotsman, James Pattle, an official in the Honourable East India Company, said to be *"the biggest liar in India"*. When he died, in 1845, his body was sent back to England in a coffin, preserved in alcohol; unfortunately this burst during a storm at sea. Mrs Pattle witnessed her dead husband's pickled body exploding from the cask, and went mad, *"raving ... the shock sent her off her head"*.

Educated in England and France, from 1818 to 1834, Julia returned to Calcutta in 1838, to marry Charles Hay Cameron. He was twenty years her senior, and a widower; they had met two years earlier at the Cape of Good Hope, while both were recuperating from illness.

Julia was greatly to help Charles Cameron, a reformer in the mould of Jeremy Bentham, in his work for the Supreme Council of India. It was here in Calcutta that she first established herself as a society hostess - despite her inbred hatred of stuffiness and convention - organising social functions for Lord Hardinge, the Governor General.

Julia herself was full of energy, but no beauty; her dark hair and olive skin reflected her French antecedents, but she was short and a prominent wart dominated the left side of her face. The oddity of her appearance was enhanced by the way in which she would festoon herself with brightly coloured shawls and drapery, the most enduring aspect of her time in India. On Charles' retirement from public life in 1848, they moved back to England, where Julia became part of the artistic community based around Little Holland House, Kensington - other prime movers included Julia's sister Sara Prinsep, the poet Henry Taylor, and the painter G.F.Watts, with occasional visits from Alfred, Lord Tennyson; Millais, Rossetti, Holman Hunt and Burne-Jones formed its Pre-Raphaelite axis.

Julia on the Island

But Julia required her own firmament in which to shine. The chance came in 1860, when she visited Tennyson at Farringford, his home at Freshwater Bay on the Isle of Wight.

Julia had first visited the Island in 1855: in a a letter of the time, she refers already to the *"dear Isle of Wight"*. Emily Tennyson's *"Journal"* relates frequent visits over the next few years. As this affinity both with poet and place deepened, Julia resolved to move to Freshwater permanently, and in 1860 she bought two adjacent cottages in Terrace Lane, Freshwater, at a strategic spot half way between Farringford and the Bay - the one to the west was called "Sunnyside" - from Jacob Long, a local fisherman.

These she joined together, linking them with a central tower - in the then fashionable "Gothic" style - to make the house look more beautiful to friends returning from the beach, re-naming the whole "Dimbola Lodge" after the family estates in Ceylon.

It was here that Cameron established a literary and artistic salon, hosting social events for Tennyson and his guests and herself bringing the Little Holland House set to this remote Island village. G.F.Watts also moved to Freshwater, along with his child bride the actress Ellen Terry, while distinguished visitors like Darwin, Thackeray, Lewis Carroll, and Edward Lear came for long summer holidays.

Anne Thackeray Ritchie described the shock of first meeting this imperious, generous, kindly, frightening eccentric, in her element as hostess.

"a strange apparation in a flowing red velvet dress, although it was summer time, cordially welcoming us to some belated meal, when the attendant butler was addressed by her as 'man' and was ordered to do many things for our benefit; to bring back the luncheon dishes and curries for which Mrs Cameron and her family had a speciality.

When we left she came with us bareheaded and trailing draperies".

But the greatest prize was Tennyson, and Julia built him a special gate - still in existence - at the back of Dimbola so that he could walk through the fields from Farringford without being bothered by the ever growing numbers of day trippers. *"Cockneys"*, he called them, and they would eventually bring an end to his hard-won solitude.

Tennyson was not the only attraction of Freshwater Bay. In a letter she wrote in 1865, Julia described the landscape in which she worked, as seen from Dimbola Lodge:

"The elms make a golden girdle around us now. The dark purple hills of England behind are a glorious picture in the morning when the sun shines on them and the elm trees

... there is something so wholesome in beauty, and it is not for me to try to tell of all we have here in those delicate tints of a distant bay and the still more distant headlands. These I see every day with my own eyes".

It was such intense concern for beauty, and visual effects, which had already turned Mrs Cameron towards the new craze for photography, in which she was to establish herself as a great artist, indeed as the creative equal of Tennyson or Watts.

Julia as a Photographer

In 1835, in the balmy atmosphere of the Cape of Good Hope, Julia had first met Sir John Herschel, then experimenting with the use of chemicals in photographic processing. Herschel was to keep her in touch with scientific progress in this field, not least the "wet collodion" process, invented by Frederick Scott Archer in 1851.

Following the chance gift of a camera by Julia Norman in 1863, during one of her husband's protracted visits to Ceylon, Mrs Cameron enthusiastically took up this new craze. In *Annals of My Glass House*, Julia relates that

"my first lens was given to me by my cherished departed daughter with the words 'It may amuse you, Mother, to try to photograph during your solitude at Freshwater'.

I handled my lens with a tender ardour, and it has become to me as a living thing, with voice and memory and creative vigour. I began with no knowledge of the art. I did not know where to place my dark box, how to focus my sitter, and my first picture I effaced to my consternation by rubbing my hand over the filmy side of the glass.

I was half way through a beautiful picture when a splutter of laughter from one of the children lost me that picture, and less ambitious now, I took one child alone, appealing to her feelings and telling her of the waste of poor Mrs Cameron's chemicals and strength if she moved. The appeal had its effect, and I now produced a picture which I called 'My First Success'."

Within a year she had begun to present her friends with albums of her work, and was elected a member of the Photographic Society in London.

It was still a painful process, both for subject - who had to sit absolutely still for as long as ten minutes - and photographer, who was not only in close contact with potentially dangerous chemicals and acids, but had to carefully manipulate light and shade, working - literally - in the dark.

Dimbola Lodge served both as her home and, more importantly, her studio. It was here that the greatest of Julia Margaret Cameron's photographs were made. It is extraordinary that she achieved such subtle tonal effects from, in effect, an old greenhouse as a studio, blanketing out certain panes to direct the available light.

However, one quality she certainly did not lack was enthusiasm. As she later described it,

"I turned my coal-house into my dark room and a glazed fowl-house I had given to my children became my glass house ... the society of hens and chickens was soon changed for that of poets, prophets, painters and lovely maidens, who all in turn have immortalised this humble little farm erection".

This dark room still survives, even if built over, as - for the moment - does Dimbola Lodge, now divided into two separate houses. The glasshouse is gone, a modern bungalow in its place. The artistic results of this burst of photographic energy - including the album we present here - still survive, and have been increasingly regarded as one of the great artistic hoards of the late 19th Century.

Onto the back lawn of Dimbola were herded - often protesting and sometimes in bizarre costume - the cream of the *"poets, prophets, painters"* of the century. Tennyson, Browning, W. M. Rossetti, Alice Liddell, Thomas Carlyle, Ellen Terry, Longfellow, G.F.Watts, Darwin, Trollope: all were cajoled to suffer for her art.

Indeed, like Watts, her artistic hero, who was attempting to paint the great Victorians to form a gallery of the age, Cameron was self-consciously recording and creating a pantheon. As Watts wrote about his own artistic methods,

"What I try for is the half-unconscious insistence of the nobilities of the subjects".

Again like Watts, Julia captured both the great and the good, along with "lovely maidens" in her own employ, in a series of posed tableaux - some sublime, some ridiculous - drawn from classical and biblical mythology.

For these purposes, the unfortunate Mr Cameron and the poet Henry Taylor - a frequent visitor - were often dressed in antique costume as elders. Friar Lawrence, King David, Prospero, King Ahasuerus, were all roles played for the camera by Taylor, in his luxuriant white beard.

From her bedroom in what is now "Cameron House", Julia would watch the main road to Freshwater Bay - Gate Lane - for willing victims to her art. The porter at Yarmouth, for example, did duty as King Arthur in a series of photographs to illustrate Tennyson's "Idylls of the King".

The adulterous Sir Lancelot was more of a problem; Cameron decided on Cardinal Vaughn, *"standing in the glow of the wintry fire, looking as he ever did, the most knightly of priests"*, but Tennyson replied, in the Catholic cleric's hearing, *"I want a face well worn with human passion"*. It is a measure of Cameron's persuasive enthusiasm that the future Archbishop of Westminster still agreed to pose as the knight.

Julia strove to picture the inner as well as the outer reality, an approach which led some contemporary reviewers to dismiss her shots as out of focus or wilfully repulsive. The Photographic News considered that

"one portrait of the Poet Laureate presents him in the the guise which would be sufficient to convict him if he were charged as a rogue and a vagabond before any bench of magistrates in the kingdom".

Cameron's own favourite picture was that of her niece, and namesake, Julia Jackson. After the early death of her first husband, Herbert Duckworth, Julia married Sir Leslie Stephen, a frequent visitor to Dimbola, and later editor of the *Dictionary of National Biography.*

The Stephens' two daughters, Virginia Woolf and Vanessa Bell, were to become leading lights of the Bloomsbury Group, and they and their friends were frequently to visit Freshwater, often staying with Anne Thackeray at the Porch, directly opposite Dimbola. Indeed, Virginia Woolf's play *Freshwater* is an affectionate spoof of her great aunt's determination to create photographic art, whatever the cost.

Freshwater ends with the Camerons leaving for Ceylon, having carefully packed their coffins. In 1875, at the peak of her fame as a photographer - the second volume of Tennyson's *"Idylls of the King"* with her photographs was newly published, she had concurrent exhibitions of her work in London and Bournemouth, and there was such a demand for her prints that the Autotype Company had been instructed to make new negatives and reissue seventy early images in red, brown and black editions - Julia did indeed leave for Ceylon.

Mary Fraser-Tytler, visiting Freshwater that fateful summer, described the scene.

"The striking of the tents of the Cameron household was full of characteristic unusualness - Mrs Cameron providing for every contingency possible, to the point of

unconscious humour.

The house was soon in a state of turmoil, their rooms piled up with packing-cases, while telegrams poured in and out, and friends came in crowds to say their farewell.

All Freshwater was wailing! rich and poor ..."

They embarked at Southampton, a cow - for fresh milk during the long sea voyage - leading the procession up the gangway, Julia showering large mounted photographs on the bemused porters in lieu of tips, saying *"take this instead as a remembrance"*.

Apart from one brief visit back to England, a time of "turmoil, sickness, sorrow, marriages and deaths", she remained in Ceylon - living in a tiny bungalow with mud walls, 4,400 feet above sea level - until her death on 26th January 1879. Her husband did not long survive her, and both are buried in a tiny churchyard high in the mountains of Ceylon, *"a dream of beauty"*.

One of Julia's last letters was to Lady Tennyson, in which she looked back proudly on her achievements; *"it is a sacred blessing which has attended my photography; it gives a pleasure to millions and a deeper happiness to very many"*.

Laura Troubridge concludes the story.

"Aunt Julia died in Ceylon, where she went at an age that made it almost a certainty that she would never come back.

Pushed by curiosity, I asked her why she was going, and she told me it was to join her sons who were working there. "Where your heart is, there is your treasure also", she added,and the words sank in, though I did not in the end understand them".

It is characteristic of this eccentric, generous, determined, aggravating, inspiring genius that her final word, uttered on her death bed on looking out across her balcony to the starry night sky should be *"beautiful"*.

The Muse-haunted Scene: Life at Dimbola

Agnes Weld quotes from a manuscript poem by Charles Hay Cameron, who shared his wife's delight in the view from their home.

"The English Channel famed in war,
The Solent sea and winding Yar
Have cut an islet, yet not quite
An islet, from the Isle of Wight,
For 'twixt the Channel famed in war
And silent sources of the Yar,
Dry land the twentieth of a mile
Unites it to the parent isle".

The river Yar rises near Freshwater Bay.

"There dwell I, fronting Afton Down,
With little Yarmouth for my nearest town.
The little Yarmouth where the Yar
Though hindered by its gathering bar
After four miles of winding reach
At length divides the yellow beach.
And meets in Solent's brine the rills
That southward flow from Hampshire's hills.
There dwell I, nowise unreproved,
By those who, loving and beloved,
Think that to them I ought to give
The remnant I have yet to live.
Nor can they cease to wonder why
I let the gusty Solent lie
'Twixt me and them, 'twixt me and all
That men "The World and Life' do call.
No idle motive hath my will inclined,
But such as well might sway an earnest mind,
Such as to all may gladly be confessed
To dwell united near the chosen nest,
And hear the Nightingale that sings unseen
In the dark ilex, on the flowr'y green
That carpets Farringford's muse-haunted scene"

As Henry Taylor wrote, Dimbola Lodge was *"a house indeed to which everyone resorted for pleasure, and in which no man, woman or child was ever known to be unwelcome"*.

It was a place where one felt fully in touch with the natural world, indolent summer days followed by moonlit walks to the Bay, a place of perpetual sunshine and fruitfulness.

Annie Thackeray described it, with

"the sense of the sea beating against the rocks below and of calm Farringford above"

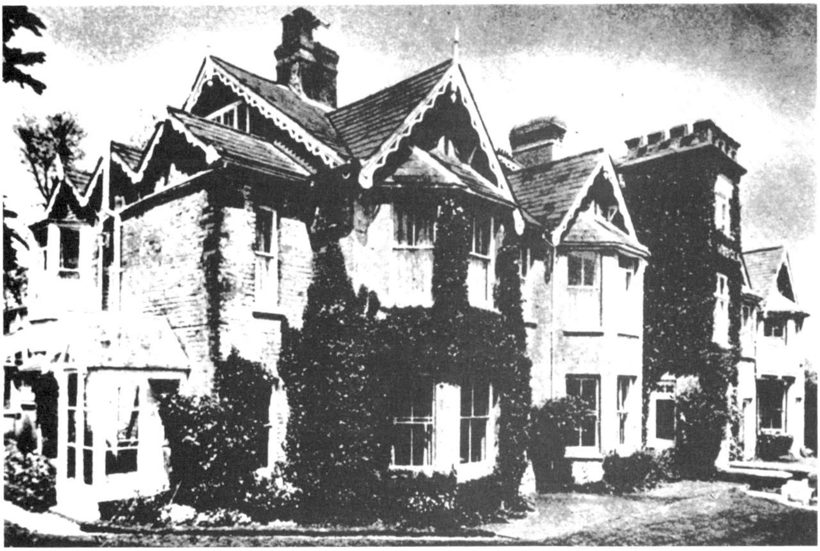

DIMBOLA LODGE

as "a true house of rest and refuge".

Agnes Weld refers to *"the picturesque, ivy-clad Dimbola, garlanded to its very roof with roses"*. Joan Brading Grayer also remembers the weight of ivy and foliage shrouding the building, which in the time she lived there was greatly reduced, in case the house collapsed.

Nevertheless, she still remembers her delight at being able to pluck a climbing rose through the open window.

Hester Fuller recalls

"Dimbola, with its smiling bay windows and low picturesque gables, stands half-way between Farringford and the sea. The house is sun-drenched, and its romantic view of the sea and rocks made it indeed a fit home for Mrs Cameron, who loved everything that was beautiful.

It was during a short visit to Farringford that one day, on a sudden impulse, she agreed to purchase a couple of houses by the roadside from a certain Jacob Long, an old sailor, who sailed the high seas and dabbled in bricks and mortar when on shore.

Jacob Long's houses were purchased and furnished, and planted with ivy and sweet briar and christened "Dimbola" after one of the Cameron estates in Ceylon.

The stories of Mrs Cameron are legion. She planted a wild briar hedge, and when a friend remonstrated that the passers-by were picking her sweet briar and that there would soon be none left, she answered: "But that is why I planted it, so that it should be picked and enjoyed".

The same altruistic impulse made her plant each year primroses on the bank which separated her house from the main road down to the sea. She built the tower so that Dimbola might look beautiful to her friends as they walked up from the shore. For the sake of beauty no effort would be spared, a cabbage field at the back of the house was turned into a lawn in an incredibly short spaceof time, so that an expected visitor should enjoy walks under the trees on soft down turf. One of the bay windows she had built in twenty-four hours, so that her friend Sir Henry Taylor on arriving might find the afternoon sunshine pouring in through his bedroom window.

Mrs Cameron photographed all day long, and at night she would organise impromptu plays and dances in the big, panelled hall, and partners would come out on to the lawn and dance under the stars. One warm, moonlight night the whole company, my mother describes, went streaming away across the fields up on to the Down. On another occasion Mrs Cameron led her guests to Farringford, striking matches as she went to light the way. On stormy nights Tennyson would come to Dimbola to fetch Mrs Cameron and they would go down to the shore together. Visitors to Dimbola should notice the green door leading into the lane at the back of the house through which Tennyson would always come. He hated to be looked at, and through this door he could avoid the publicity of the road down to the Bay."

Survivals

Tennyson's gate in Back Lane is still in existence, though it is not the original door.

Julia's studio was demolished in 1928; a modern bungalow now stands in its place. The darkroom is still in existence, built over as a larder. The rinsing sinks also turned up elsewhere.

Eric Toogood recalls how some of the large glass plates were used as garden cloches in a house in Southdown Road, and how some were used as roof lights in Dimbola/Cameron House itself.

Many of the original features which obtrude into Cameron's photographs still exist - for example the decorative iron work, French windows and tradesman's entrance of what is now "Cameron House" can still be recognised.

Dimbola Lodge was subsequently divided into two (adjoining) properties, "Cameron House" and "Dimbola", the latter now fronted by a glass conservatory. All attempts to list these two buildings have so far failed, and "Cameron House" could well be demolished by the time this book is published.

Otherwise accurate accounts of Mrs Cameron's life and work continue to relate the quite erroneous information that the "Cameron House" side of "Dimbola Lodge" was never lived in by the Camerons but merely used as accommodation for her guests.

There are two reasons for this fallacy. Firstly, several contemporary accounts refer to Mrs Cameron's "guest cottage". This is undoubtedly the "Porch", destroyed by a German action, but on the other side of the road to "Dimbola Lodge", in the Square.Secondly, Agnes Weld quotes Sir John Simeon's daughter Louisa, presumably from a letter

"The autumn and winter of 1871-72 my eldest brother and I spent together at Freshwater. We rented Mrs Cameron's little house, which opens by a door of communication into the large hall of Dimbola, the house in which she lived.

The evening we arrived she suddenly appeared in our drawing room, saying "When strangers take this house, I keep the door between us locked - with friends never"; and locked it never was.

We lived almost as part of the family, and it was a real enjoyment to be in such close intimacy with one of the most original and at the same time tender-hearted and generous women I have ever known".

This is not as conclusive as it first appears. Note the late date, by which time Mrs Cameron's family were mostly grown up, and some of her sons were already working in

Ceylon. Note also the continuance of a "door of communication".

The most startling evidence to recently emerge was the account by Mrs Joan Brading Grayer of a childhood spent in the original "Dimbola Lodge".

Mrs Grayer and her family were the last people to live there before it was again split into two separate properties. Her parents bought Dimbola from the Elliot family, who had themselves preserved it, virtually intact, as it was at Mrs Cameron's departure in 1875.

From her own childhood memories, and long discussions she had with Hester Thackeray Fuller, Mrs Grayer has pieced together the plan of the original "Dimbola Lodge".

With her kind permission, I will quote briefly from Mrs Grayer's account, soon to be published in its own right. Certainly, Mrs Grayer's new evidence radically enhances our knowledge of Mrs Cameron's sojourn at Freshwater.

When Mrs Cameron bought these two double-fronted bay windowed houses, she joined them together with a castellated tower, covered with white climbing roses. Mrs Grayer:

"Myrtle and sweet briar bushes graced the base of the four bay windows which looked out upon a red-tiled terrace on either side of the tower, parted by a graceful flight of steps leading to the front door".

The main hall was approached by the steps into the tower; its doorways were richly carved, as was the wide staircase, branching to the east and west wings. Annie Thackeray recalls

"In those days Mrs Cameron seemed to be omnipresent. Of an evening came impromptu plays and waltzes in the wooden ballroom, and young partners dancing out under the stars.

One warm moonlight night I remember the whole company of lads and lasses went streaming away across fields and downs, past silvery sheepfolds to the very cliffs overhanging the sea".

To the west of the tower, two large rooms had been knocked into one to form the drawing room. It was here that the likes of Darwin, Ruskin, Herschel, Holman Hunt, Millais, Edward Lear and Thackeray would repair after dinner, and that Mr Cameron would walk up and down, reciting Homer aloud, *'a philosopher with his beard dipped in moonlight'* as Tennyson once described him.

In the "Cameron House" side of the house, downstairs nearest to the main road, were the dining room and the study. On the floor above, at the back of the house, was Mrs Cameron's bedroom. As Mrs Grayer writes,

"Not only was it within sight of the 'Tennyson' gate through which the poet would make his almost secret entrance to the Dimbola garden, but the other window to the north overlooked the main road to the beach. It is said that she would watch out for any good-looking person passing along the road to the shore, and send her maid to beg of them to come and pose before her camera".

On the first floor of what is now "Dimbola" is the bedroom where Ellen Terry stayed, when she was a bride of sixteen. Her room looked out across the fields, golden with corn, to wide open views of the Bay.

The house was surrounded by extensive grounds, its boundary with the lane behind guarded by a high brick wall. Besides the lawn on which Julia's glass house stood, the highlight of the garden was a rustic bridge. As Mrs Grayer remembers,

"The bridge was the highlight of the garden. This pretty walk consisted of a high bank approached by a flight of stone steps near to which was a rare 'Judas Tree', like a pink jewel on the green lawn."

West Wight Connections

To the Island

Visitors from London would take the train to Brockenhurst, whose waiting room was filled with original Cameron prints,

" This gallery of the great men of our age is presented for this room by Mrs Cameron in grateful memory of this being the spot where she first met one of her sons after a long absence of four years in Ceylon",

then a horse carriage to Lymington, where they would board a steam packet.

The very crossing to the Island - lying "like a waterlily on a blue lake" as Tennyson described it - seemed to be to a magical world, where the constraints of the metropolis were cast aside, and art was all.

The painter Holman Hunt, writing to Emily Tennyson after a stay at Freshwater, remarked that *"my holiday brought balm and health to me, and I went back to my work with renewed zest."*

By the 1850s, the towns of Cowes, Ryde and Newport were relatively easy to reach by sea, but access to Freshwater depended very much on the irregular sailings of a little vessel crossing the Solent at Yarmouth, "which when it crossed", said a resident of the time, "we got letters, and when it did not cross we went without". If visitors missed the ferry, they could take a rowing boat.

It was between Lymington and Yarmouth that Tennyson wrote *Crossing the Bar* on the back of an envelope; one author even names the boat, the *Mayflower.*

Visitors would embark at Yarmouth Pier; to whose waiting room, now a tea bar, Cameron had again donated a display of photographs of famous local subjects.

From here, visitors were conveyed in a two-horse coach to Freshwater, or walked through the fields. On their return to Yarmouth, they were directed with the cry "This way for England".

Change in the Village

The growth of Freshwater as a popular resort was rapid. Charles Tennyson describes the village in the 1850s, shortly before the Camerons arrived;

"a few small houses and a little white hotel by the Bay, a few more houses clustered round the old church by the river, and sparsely scattered about the winding lanes 'of elm and whispering oak' old stone cottages and seventeenth century farms with roofs of thatch or stone tiling".

Less than ten years after they left, a local guide reports

"Freshwater Bay is a rising and fashionable watering place, the facility for bathing being rapidly extended".

White's *Directory* of 1859 lists mainly farmers, blacksmiths, grocers, and wheelwrights, along with a few inns and taverns. The only profession of note, other than "gentleman" or "Poet Laureate", are those of gunner and light house keeper. Hill's

Directory of 1879 lists a profusion of "furnished apartments" for rent; the new arrivals include insurance agents, dissenting ministers, second home owners - including, by now, the Poet Laureate - photographers and surgeons.

The sheer growth in the list of residents - and their newly built properties - is startling. The spread of these holiday villas surely inspired Tennyson's lines,

"Yonder lies our young sea-village - Art and Grace are less and less
Science grows and beauty dwindles - roofs of slated hideousness!"

Tennyson would decamp to Aldworth, remote on a hillside on the Hampshire /Surrey border, to escape these summer visitors.

One reason for this sudden growth in popularity was the Victorian craze for the sea; early photographs of the Bay show bathing machines and a strange brick-built sea bathing hut, with both hot and cold receptacles.

Another factor was the coming of the railways, whose extension to the Bay Tennyson successfully prevented - *"the threatened railway with a terminus at the Bay is to be stopt at Hook Hill or Pound Green. Not welcome to us even then"!*, as Emily recorded in her Journal for March 1865.

A further reason for this influx of tourists was the very fame which Queen Victoria and Tennyson himself brought to the Isle of Wight. The introduction in 1871 of statutory Bank Holidays meant that working people were able to visit the Island as day trippers. These were the "cockneys" who so annoyed the poet, but whose purchase of cheap editions of his work made him so rich.

As compared to Mrs Cameron, who turned the giving of presents into a mania, Tennyson was notoriously mindful of his royalties, and willing to desert his original publisher if it suited him financially!

By some irony, the spectre of development has again come to haunt the Bay. This time, under threat are the very holiday villas which Tennyson so hated - by and large the more ancient farmhouses and cottages are now protected.

One of the things I hope to show in the current study is how important and interconnected a community Freshwater Bay was at the time of Cameron, Tennyson and Watts and how, miraculously, most of this fabric is still intact. One can still see the views they saw, drive past the houses they lived in, take the same country paths they walked.

I would certainly argue the urgent need for conservation of this time capsule of Victoriana. Architecturally an interesting but not unique development, artistically and historically it forms a unified whole, the testimony in stone, slate, bricks and mortar of this attempt to recreate Periclean Athens in Victorian England.

As Miss Stephen exclaimed at the time: *"Is there no-one who is commonplace here? Is everybody either a poet, or a genius, or a painter, or peculiar in some way?"*.

Anne Thackeray captured the reason for such artistic riches;

"Freshwater in the 1860s and 1870s was unique, for not only was it an enchanting place in itself with high downs, glorious views of the English Channel and air "worth sixpence a pint" as Tennyson wrote to a friend, but a delightful company of people had come to live there to be near their friend Tennyson".

And Julia Cameron was on hand to immortalise them with her camera.

I will briefly try to trace this web of connections and history, through the Victorian residences of Freshwater Bay.

THE BAY

The Bay has long attracted artists; Turner, George Morland, John Martin, John Nixon,

Augustus John, G.F.Watts and, on one of her only visits to England, the French Impressionist Berthe Morisot.

This is surely the setting for Tennyson's *Enoch Arden*;

"Long lines of cliff breaking have left a chasm;
And in the chasm are foam and yellow sands"

Like memories of the great Victorians, the sands have ebbed in recent years! Tennyson said of the same poem that in one particular line, *"The League-long roller thundering on the reef"* he had captured *"the sound of the sea"*.

Of the same bay, Professor Tyndall wrote,

"I sat near the shore observing the advance of the waves and listening to their thunder. The pebbles and shingles on the beach are mainly flint, and emit a sharp sound on collision with each other. As the billows break and roll up the beach they carry the shingle along with them, and on their retreat they drag it downwards.

Here the collision of the flint pebbles are innumerable. They blend together in a continuous sound which could not be better described than by the line in "Maud" (much criticised by reviewers) "Now to the scream of a madden'd beach drag'd down by the wave".

Hester Fuller adds, in *Three Freshwater Friends*,

"In 'Geraint and Enid', I always think that the dress which Earl Doorm offered Enid, is like our sea at Freshwater on a calm summer day,
'Where, like a shoaling sea, the lovely blue
Play'd into green'."

In contrast, but equally true to those who know Freshwater Bay in all seasons is a line from *Sea Dreams*: 'The sea roars ruin: a fearful night'!"

Indeed, Freshwater Bay - and the whole shoreline from the Needles down to Blackgang - remained a dangerous and unforgiving place, part indeed of its attraction for the poet. Emily Tennyson's *Journal* contains a catalogue of disasters. In December 1872, she records

"a fearful storm and shipwreck. The tarbarrel & lights are seen to burn a few minutes or a quarter of an hour as some say and wild cries are heard or fancied & then all is silent and dark. A board floats in with 'The Hope' on it. Every soul on board has perished within sight of many on shore".

Again, William Allingham recounts, five years earlier:

"Walk with T. to Brook Bay, ship ashore, the 'Fannie Larabee' of Bath,large three masts, good model. There are people on the shore, but T. doesn't seem to mind. We walked to next pointand saw a steamer ashore at Atherfield; then turned up to downs and came back by a path slanting along the cliff side, like a frightful dream rather, my head being lightish.

T tells of people who have fallen over, and at one place is a monumental stone to commemmorate such an accident. I said (walking close behind him) 'suppose I were to slip and catch hold of you, and we both rolled down together' on which T. stopped and said, 'you'd better go first".

The memorial to the unfortunate girl thus to take an early plunge - with its reassuring motto, *In the midst of life we are in death* to cheer the casual walker, is still in place.

In October 1868, Allingham records a walk by the newly built *"Military Road"*, tracing the same route in reverse, and perhaps even including among the party Nellie Mundy herself, to whom the IWCC album is dedicated:

"We find the Tennyson carriage at Miss Thackeray's; Mrs T. asks the ladies, 'Will you take compassion on him?' that is allow A.T. to walk with them and they do consent.

A.T. comes accordingly, and we walk off (Mrs R., Miss Augusta, Miss Emily, Nellie, Miss Annie Prinsep, A.T. and W.A.) down old road, by Afton Park fence, field-path through turnips to Afton Down, see the barrows (ancient burial mounds), cross the rough new military road, and by path to shore; geology - Wealden; so on to Brook Point and the fossil trees.

T. (enjoying the girls' company) says; 'If I could take a walk like this every day I shouldn't be tired of Freshwater'".

GLENBROOK later known as GLENBROOK ST FRANCIS

Now renamed "Promenade Holiday Flats", and divided into separate apartments, Glenbrook overlooks the Bay, where it is situated directly above the Inshore Rescue station.

Glenbrook served as the Dower House of Lady May Tennyson - the second wife of the poet's son Hallam.

As May Prinsep, she had been brought up at Little Holland House, and was much photographed by Julia Cameron on her frequent visits to Freshwater, where she stayed first at Dimbola and later at the Briary.

The most distinguished guest between the wars was Haile Selassie, the Emperor of Ethiopia and then in exile, who would walk with his retinue down the middle of the road, confident that no motorist would dare harm his imperial majesty. Selassie was later canonised by Jamaican rastafarians - including Bob Marley - as the Lion of Judah, the mystical leader of black Africa.

Later, Colonel Prinsep, descendent of Val Prinsep - who had stayed at the Briary with his friend G.F.Watts - lived here, apparently with a Russian princess. He later committed suicide.

This is perhaps the Evelyn Prinsep whose *Freshwater Gates; a Miscellany* was privately published from Glenbrook - St Francis, dated Christmas 1945, and printed by the *County Press.*

The title poem at least is still relevant.

"Between the Needles and Black Gang
The hand of man is barely seen;
And this is where great poet sang
His "Idylls of the King" to Queen

But where the hand of man has been
Was beauty's knell by fashion rung,
By bricks and mortar like a fung-
Us, hideous growth on sylvan sheen."

FORT REDOUBT

Built to defend the Bay from French attack. The children of its Master Gunner, Thomas Keown, provided photographic models for Mrs Cameron.

PLUMLEYS HOTEL

Now owned by the Holiday Fellowship; it overlooks the Bay.

When George Morland stayed here in 1799, it was called the "George Inn", and kept by a Mr Plumley. Morland was hiding from his creditors; but a sketching trip to Yarmouth brought disaster.

"One fine drawing in particular, although it was only a spaniel dog in a landscape,

was construed by the honest lieutenant into the plan of the island, and the dog, he was confident, represented the very part of it upon which the enemy were to land."

The same inn was later known as Lamberts and Freshwater Bay Hotel. Anthony Trollope and "Lewis Carroll" were just two of the many famous guests to stay there.

OCEAN VIEW

Christopher Isherwood and Edward Upward, friends from Cambridge, lodged here in the mid 1920s, and were visited by W.H.Auden with whom they would sing hymns in the evening, to Auden's fierce piano accompaniment.

Isherwood records the Victorian decor of the house in *Lions and Shadows*, his fictional autobiography, with a kind of amused horror;

"Nothing had been moved. The frosted glass lamp still stood in th middle of the table cloth with the woollen pom poms. The Maiden's Prayer still hung over the fireplace, and above the piano was the photograph of Lord Tennyson, described by the poet as "the Dirty Monk". How happy I felt, in this room".

One wonders if this Cameron print was an original. In *August for the people and their favourite islands*, Auden too looks back, in a poem dedicated to Isherwood, to a time when all seemed possible, when art was all;

"Nine years ago, upon that southern island
Where the wild Tennyson became a fossil,
Half-boys, we spoke of books and praised
The acid and austere, behind us only
The stuccoed suburb and expensive school.
Scented our turf, the distant baying
Nice decoration to the artist's wish;
Yet fast the deer was flying through the wood".

THE ALBION HOTEL

Turner stayed here, on a youthful sketching trip of the Bay. His first watercolour is a view of boats off the Needles.

A favourite resort of the artist George Morland (1763-1804), when it was a small public house called the "Cabin". Here he was to be found consorting with smugglers, sailors, fishermen and poachers, who became the subjects of his work. As Morland himself said. *"Where could I find such a picture of life as that* (exhibiting his sketch book) *unless among the originals of the Cabin?"*

Morland also consorted at a nearby inn called the "Mermaid". As Plumleys became more grand, the Albion retained its raffish atmosphere, although in Cameron's time it had become known as the "Royal Albion", and was presumably much used by the fort keepers at Fort Redoubt.

In the 1950s, J.B.Priestley would drink here, with his wife the archaeologist Jacquetta Hawkes, and guests - including the historian A.J.P.Taylor and the poet Louis Macneice - and treat them to *"Dog's Nose"*. This he himself described as *"an old mixture of gin and draught ale, not intended for the sedentary"*.

BEACH HOUSE

Later Afton Down Hotel, now divided into flats under its original name; Lord Bryce regularly stayed here. Hester Fuller quotes a letter from William Allingham to Madame de la Tour,

"It is highly interesting to hear of John Milton's descendants in Beach House,

especially as my friend Mrs Tennant and her daughters, living under the same roof, are lineal descendants of Oliver Cromwell".

BAKER'S FARM

A listed building, grade III, built about 1514. Behind are the remains of ancient barns. It was with the Bakers that Mrs Cameron travelled when she left Freshwater for Ceylon in 1875.

STARKS HOTEL

A gazetteer refers to Mrs Stark of St Catherine's View, Freshwater Gate, as taking in paying guests. Mr Stark is named as the hirer of coaches and conveyances, a kind of horse drawn taxi service; (the stables were behind Plumley's hotel).

Emily Tennyson's *Journal* for January 1869 records Alfred seeing about *"the road for which Starks wishes"*, perhaps Guyers Road?

THE MALL

Opposite Baker's Farm. The shops here were built to service the new Victorian residents of Freshwater, including an apocathary, and - at the turn of the century - Mr Gubbins, official piano tuner to Queen Victoria. He ran a library agency, while on the forecourt he hired out basinettes to visitors.

This in turn became "Woolf and Geer", a local booksellers and newsagents established by two cousins who moved to Freshwater in 1929. The descendants of Alfred, Lord Tennyson often visited this shop, Miss Geer in particular became a close friend of the later Tennysons, and a fund of local knowledge.

Part of this shop is now Freshwater Bay Post Office.

ST AGNES

Thatched church, built from ancient stone from a ruined building on Hooke Hill - local rumour has it that they came from the cottage in which the scientist Robert Hooke was born. The carved date 1694, incorporated in the vestry wall, comes from this original building.

In fact the church was built early this century, to replace the "Iron Room" in the Square, which was now too small to contain the congregation.

Hallam Tennyson, the poet's son, donated the land on which it stood from the Tennyson estate, as he wished to establish a local place of worship. Lady Tennyson suggested the church be dedicated to Saint Agnes, and gave the church porch in memory of her mother.

The foundation stone was laid by Harold Tennyson in 1908.

There are interesting memorials to the Tennyson family and their friends, including Anne Thackeray.

Further along Gate Lane is the start of "Farringford Lane", the original main drive to Farringford, which runs up to the rustic bridge.

The Russian novelist Turgenev is later recorded as walking the local lanes, without meeting Alfred - he did so at Aldworth - as is the Jesuit poet Gerald Manley Hopkins.

ORCHARDS

First erected about 1845 as a private dwelling; it was first opened as a village shop by Mr Orchard in 1865, as still proudly painted above the front door. Its architectural importance lies in its being built at that date in the most modern style, and remaining unaltered to the present day.

To the left was the bakehouse, and to the right the original Post Office; the store itself sold food, oil, coal, wines and spirits and attracted many famous customers. On one memorable occasion fellow poets Tennyson and the American Henry Wadsworth Longfellow were both there at the same time!

WHITECLIFF HOUSE

The Liddell family stayed here, with their daughter Alice, immortalised both as the heroine of Alice in Wonderland and in Julia Cameron's photographs "Pomona", "St Agnes" and "Alethia".

She was very much part of the Tennyson circle. Hester Thackeray Fuller records that *"Mrs Cameron also photographed "Alice in Wonderland" who came with her sisters and her father, Dean Liddle, to stay at Freshwater one summer".*

MONKSFIELD

In the early part of the 20th Century, the painter Augustus John stayed here with the Slade family, associated with the famous art school in London, and made sketching trips to the Bay.

HOLLY TREE COTTAGE

According to some local historians, the Revd Dodgson stayed here, opposite Whitecliff House, and one witness even asserts that here was where, as "Lewis Carroll" he wrote part of "Alice in Wonderland".

MYRTLE COTTAGE

The lodgings of William Allingham when he came over from Lymington to visit Tennyson and Mrs Cameron. His wife, the painter Helen Allingham produced many fine images of local farmhouses and cottages, as well as some detailed paintings of Farringford.

Mrs Clough, widow of the poet, also stayed here. Mrs Cameron wrote a poem of condolence to her remembering Arthur Hugh Clough's last visit to Freshwater;

"But eighteen months ago - and here he stood
Warm as the summer air in fullest June
Pouring all learning like a golden flood -
Now - all is vanished - too soon - too soon"

Julia captures in this poem Clough's religious doubts and tragic nature, *"the tender questionings of a wild unrest/of noble soul".*

HAZLEHURST

"On the left hand from the Dimbola Hotel stands "Hazlehurst" under whose hospitable roof so many celebrities have stayed. Mrs Calloway's memories go back to Tennyson and Mrs Cameron, for whom she often posed for camera pictures".

Hester Thackeray Fuller, *Three Freshwater Friends* (1933).

HAVELOCK

A strange iron building, behind Havelock and now demolished, served as Sunday school and local church, before the construction of St Agnes.

This could well have been due to the beneficence of Mrs Cameron, and might indeed have been the reading room which she donated to the village, lying as it did within close proximity to Dimbola Lodge.

THE PORCH (since destroyed)

On the other side of the Square facing Havelock, and adjoining Hazlehurst. Now replaced by two modern semi-detached cottages.

The Porch was built originally for Benjamin Jowett the classicist, who was working on his edition of Plato, to whom its name alludes. It did indeed have a porch, but the reference is to the ideal Athenian intellectual society - the arts and sciences as one - to which the Freshwater circle aspired.

Anne and Minnie Thackeray, daughters of the novelist, took up residence in 1863, following the death of their father. When they returned from his funeral, they looked out to see Tennyson standing outside their front window, in his black cloak, as a silent but perhaps unsettling mark of respect. In her Journal, Anne wrote,

"This sad year began at Freshwater. It was bitter weather. Minny and I were at Mrs Cameron's cottage. She was goodness in person. Alfred Tennyson used to come and see us in his cloak".

Though currently neglected as a writer, as Laura Troubridge recalls

"Annie Thackeray, afterwards Lady Ritchie, flashes across these memories of Freshwater and Dimbola, for she was more than welcome at both houses. She was, as everybody knows, a daughter of the great William Makepeace Thackeray, and inherited much of his talent as a writer, and even a sweet, pale reflection of his genius who was taking notes indeed. Those eyes, at once shrewd and kind, noted, as we knew, all the eccentricities of Mrs Prinsep and Mrs Cameron, and their eager, somewhat un-English way of life, and one is not surprised, in her Memoirs, to come across some amusing descriptions of it all just touched in with a sure hand.

They too, laughed at her, though they loved her; for she was utterly oblivious to clothes and in Mrs Prinsep's eyes that was almost a sin. She was forgetful and unpunctual, and in some ways not unlike the White Queen in "Alice in Wonderland". Still, in spite of their respective peculiarities, I cannot help thinking these women lived on a higher plane than most women seem to do now."

Anne Thackeray herself has left the best description in print of her second home, capturing the dream-like atmosphere of the Bay.

"This is the Porch, the gate of heaven. There is a sense of repose that I think one must feel after death before beginning the new life. (It is inconceivable how I enjoy it. I do nothing for hours together). The sitting room opens into a tiny conservatory, and through an open window one hears the enchanted moan of the sea and the song of the birds.

I wake at six and hear the earliest pipe of half-awakened birds, and I go to sleep with the sea in my ears and a star looking in at my window".

Virginia Woolf stayed at the Porch with Annie Thackeray while recovering from one of a series of nervous breakdowns, and was to satirise the Victorian inhabitants of the Bay in her privately performed drama *Freshwater*.

Woolf's parents, Leslie Stephen and Julia Duckworth, had met at a ball held by Mrs Cameron - Julia's aunt - at Dimbola Lodge.

Hester Fuller writes in *Three Freshwater Friends;*

"Next door to Mrs Calloways's house is "The Porch", a little cottage which, when built by Mrs Cameron, stood in the fields. It was christened "The Porch" by Mrs Cameron

after the celebrated Athenian Porch where Socrates and Plato held forth to admiring crowds. Jowett was at this time translating Plato, and Mrs Cameron built "The Porch" for him, in which to work and stay.

The appearance of the cottage has been altered since the creepers were pulled down and the Porch itself taken away. It was here that my mother (Anne Thackeray) came constantly to stay before her marriage, and here for many years we spent happy holidays, and during the war made the cottage our permanent home".

The Porch was destroyed by a German bomb during the 2nd World War. Mrs Grayer relates how *"some of the debris had fallen on Dimbola, including a five foot long beam, which embedded itself on top of the tower, like a crooked flagpole".*

TERRACE HOUSE

Tennyson's Dower House, originally a smugglers cottage. The poet first bought it to keep it undeveloped, and his views from Farringford open. Later he leased it to his younger brother Horatio, whose name appears in the 1871 Gazetteer for Freshwater as resident there.

Agnes Weld writes of him, *"never was a man better fitted than him to make an ideal parish priest, yet he never could be persuaded to think himself worthy of becoming a clergyman, and so his magnificent voice was only heard in lay ministry at the bedsides of the sick and the dying ... to whom he would insist on carrying off any special dainty intended for his own dinner - a meal which he would constantly omit to come home to - his hunger forgotten".*

Hester Fuller writes

"The Terrace House with the handsome iron gates at the end of the road is the property of the Tennyson family, and is interesting for its garden and its most beautiful views of the English Channel and the remembrance that Jowett of Oxford fame came here Spring after Spring to be near his friend the Poet".

THE PANNELLS (originally ST CATHERINE'S HOUSE).

Summer home of the novelist William Makepiece Thackeray, and renamed after the Anglo-Saxon "pannell" of land. After her father's death, Anne Thackeray, a late-Victorian novelist much admired by Virginia Woolf, moved to the Porch.

"The house next to Redoubt was built for Tennyson's brother Frederick. Many interesting people have in turn stayed here. Dean Bradley, the famous Dean of Westminster, Leslie Stephen the critic, his sister the mystic(?), my mother the writer (Anne Thackeray).

The house was christened Pannells by Hallam Lord Tennyson. In the old charters of the Farringford estate as far back as the 12th century, the land on which the house stands was known as "Pannells" which means a small patch of ground".

Hester Fuller, *Three Freshwater Friends*

Another lodger here was the poet Philip Stanhope Worsley, who produced what Matthew Arnold considered some of the best translations of Homer, and who died young, of consumption, despite Mrs Cameron's devoted nursing.

REDOUBT HOUSE

Charles Darwin the great naturalist came here, in precarious health, in the summer of 1869. William Allingham describes him as *"yellow, sickly, very quiet".* Darwin's daughter, however, records that *"it was a beautiful summer and we had a very entertaining time. Mrs Cameron was most amusing and put my father and Erasmus Darwin, who was with us, into great spirits".*

Alfred Tennyson, who had prefigured the Origin of Species in *In Memoriam*, was reassured to find him

"very kindly, unworldly and agreeable. A. said to him, 'Your theory of Evolution does not make against Christianity': and Darwin answered 'No, certainly not'".

Darwin was captured by Mrs Cameron, and wrote of the resulting portrait, *"I like this photograph very much better than any other which has been taken of me".*

Hester Fuller writes of these times,

"It was in 1860 that Darwin came with his family to Freshwater, and it was then that his photograph was taken. When Darwin wrote to Mrs Cameron approving of the portrait he said "There are sixteen people in my house and every one is your friend." The Darwins stayed at Redoubt House next door to Dimbola for the summer. Darwin brought his horse with him. Darwin's daughter told me the story of the horse and how her father rode up on to Afton Down the first morning and let the reins drop to see what his steed would do. The horse paused for a moment and then went straight off in the direction of Down, Darwin's home, from whence they had all come.

Redoubt House can boast of another famous guest, Jenny Lind, "The Swedish Nightingale," the most famous of prima donnas. Musicians will be interested to know that at Farringford is the little upright piano on which the singer accompanied herself when she sang to Tennyson".

This piano now resides at the Tennyson Research Centre, Lincoln, along with the poet's library and many keepsakes, transferred from Farringford.

Emily Tennyson records in her *Journal* of May 12th 1871 that Madame Goldschmidt (Jenny Lind) dines at Farringford, and sings two special requests of the poet's, *"Auld Lang Syne"* and *"Auld Robin Gray"*, as well as some Handel and two Swedish songs *"which show her voice off wonderfully".*

When Jenny Lind was practising her scales at Redoubt House, her voice was so penetrating it could be clearly heard by fishermen down in the bay!

FARRINGFORD HOUSE

Hester Fuller writes:

"Farringford was Tennyson's home for thirty-nine years. The story is well known of how the Poet and his wife one November evening rowed across the Solent in an open boat and "one dark heron flew over the sea, backed by a daffodil sky". They came to Farringford and found there all the loveliness and beauty they had been looking for ever since they first married. The glorious view of Afton Down from the drawing-room window, and the lovely views of the English Channel through the elms and chestnut trees, decided them that they had come to the ideal place in which to live. The trees have grown higher and thicker, a few have lately been cut down, but except for that Farringford remains practically the same as it was eighty years ago when the Poet first came".

As Tennyson was himself to write to the Revd F.D.Maurice;

"…. far from noise and smoke of town
I watch the twilight falling brown
All round a careless-order'd garden,
Close to the ridge of a noble down."

At the end of the 2nd World War, Thomas Cook & Son bought the house, enlarged it, and reopened it as a luxury hotel; Dame Myra Hess was a frequent visitor, as was John Betjeman.

It is now owned by Sir Fred Pontin, and the precious artefacts that remained were either carefully displayed in the new study, or sent for safe keeping to the Tennyson Research Centre, Lincoln.

ROSEBERRY LODGE

James Rogers, a friend of Tennyson and a noted naturalist, came to live here in about 1845. He travelled to the Brazilian jungle on behalf of Lord Roseberry, thus the name of the house.

His descendant, the local painter Muriel Owen, still owns two rare Cameron portraits of her great great grandfather.

FARRINGFORD LODGE

Directly opposite the main entrance gates to Farringford; this was was the home of Mr Waters, butler to his lordship.

Alongside Farringford Lodge runs a footpath known as *"Granny's Mead"*, leading across the fields to Pound Green. This may well have taken its name from Granny Groves - photographed by Cameron - who lived on the Farringford estate, and survived well into her ninetieth year.

It was at Pound Green that Mary Hillier, Cameron's maid and photographic model, was born in 1847.

FARRINGFORD FARM

Always known as "Home Farm" by Tennyson, and much painted by Helen Allingham. Close to the dairy, and thus a door into the kitchen garden which forms the setting for one of Allingham's most famous pictures. Her book *The Cottage Homes of England* drew partly on the picturesque but decaying farm buildings of Freshwater.

Indeed some now form the conservation area based around Middleton (also once part of the Tennyson estate).

George Napier comments that

"the Home Farm, with its thatched roof and "martin-haunted eaves", may be taken as a type of those picturesque abodes, whose simple rusticity strikes the traveller, when he contrasts it with the shoddiness of the more pretentious villas which mar the landscape of other parts of the parish, making him wish for older times,

'When man knew how to build'".

Near the farm, set into a stone wall fronting "Locksley Hall", was the post box which the poet used to send off his poems and correspondence to the mainland. Locksley Hall is long gone, but the post box, with its fine VR plate - was saved, and is now in the care of the Parish Council.

HIGH DOWN, now TENNYSON DOWN

Hester Fuller;

"It was on High Down that Tennyson's poem "The Charge of the Light Brigade" came to him suddenly. The poem was printed as a fly-leaf and sent out to the Crimea, 1854, for the soldiers to read"

The poet would walk up to the top of High Down from Farringford every morning, sometimes pushing Emily, sometimes with a young female companion! Towards the end of his life, he would be followed by a weird procession of the reverential and the curious.

William Allingham best captured its aspect in winter - *"I go up to the Downs alone, to Beacon; wide sea, misty landscape, western light, melancholy"*.

Tennyson's favourite walk was along the top of the Down to the Needles, described a century later by John Betjeman as *"like a thrilling and terrifying dream"*.

On the highest point of the Down, 483 feet above sea level, stood Farringford Beacon, a landmark for miles around which also was used as a kind of "visitors book". Its wooden supports, and even the turf around, were cut and carved with the names of the Poet's admirers.

In 1897, this was replaced with Tennyson's Cross, made of Cornish granite and to a Celtic design. This was the choice of the poet's son Hallam; unveiled on the poet's birthday, August 6th, by the Dean of Westminster. It bears the following inscription:

In memory of Alfred Lord Tennyson This Cross is raised, a Beacon to Sailors, By the People of Freshwater and other friends in England and America

Hallam Tennyson later gave the Down to the nation, in tribute to his father's memory.

WATCOMBE BAY

On the approach to the Down from Freshwater Bay, past Plumley's Hotel, Arthur Paterson records Hallam pointing out a niche in the cliff side which was one of Alfred's favourite resting places, *"one where he would often sit, sheltered from the cold winds, gazing seawards"*.

It is likely that this is the cliff situated directly above Watcombe Bay, now inaccessible, except at low tide. Agnes Weld recalls

"when walking one day along the top of Watcombe Bay - that picturesque little cove dear to Tennyson from a sense of his Lord of the Manorship over it as well as from its own beauty - my uncle stopped suddenly to point out the sunlight gilding to a deeper golden shade the fragile rock cistus bloom at his feet and, tenderly plucking the delicate flower, he held it lovingly in his hand, and, looking up, said "There is not a flower on all this Down that owes to the sun what I owe to Christ".

Elsewhere, Tennyson sternly forbade the picking of wild flowers on his property!

It was to Watcombe Bay that Tennyson walked with a young lady whom he had rescued from Mrs Cameron's photographic studio.

"He gave her his hand to help her down the steep path into Watcombe Bay, of which he was extremely proud, and he showed her all the wealth of minute animal life that fills its limpid rock-pools.

As they gained the summit of High Down, he brought to her mind's eye a graphic picture of the geological changes that have taken place in the extensive landscape upon which they looked, and then brought her back to the life-history of the tiny mollusc, half-hidden in the short turf upon which they were treading".

MIDDLETON

The Tennysons took a great deal of interest in what happened on their farms, of which Middleton was the most productive. Alfred would himself often help in the fields, at harvest time.

Emily's *Journal* for August 1856 captures the idyllic side of all this hard toil;

"Alfred and the boys take me to see the reapers reaping winter barley & oats at Middleton - these pleasant breezy fields of ours. The day after they take me to look in at the drilling of turnips in the Withy field. The horses look fine drilling and harrowing.

A peaceful, happy time".

SHEPHERD PAUL'S COTTAGE,

Agnes Weld records, *"frequent were the visits we paid together to the cottage of Tennyson's old shepherd, and still more frequently did we watch him as he called out by name the various members of his master's flock".*

WILLIAM KNIGHT

Also pensioned off on the Tennyson estate, where he dined *"on hard boiled eggs, cooked fifty at a time, and on dried goat's flesh"* lived William Knight, a coachman who started work shortly after the Tennysons' arrival, and survived - well past eighty - the Great War.

Lionel - the poet's grandson, and England cricket captain - reported that

"Of other human beings he was scornful and contemptuous, but he considered all Tennysons the noblest and wisest people on earth."

FARM COTTAGES

Two of the cottages on the left hand side of the road leading up to Weston Manor (now known as Middleton Farm Cottages) have Tennyson's initials, AT, engraved in terra cotta onto their porches and above their downstair windows.

As George Napier writes,

"returning from the Needles, we at once know when we are within the marches of the poet's estate from the many neat little cottages peeping out amid bowers of honeysuckle, with a monogram of the letters A.E.T (Alfred and Emily Tennyson) cut in a red stone over the doorway.

"Labourers homes", "each a nest in bloom", as Tennyson's Edith Aylmer delights to visit when on her rounds of mercy".

Agnes Weld adds further detail.

"He had an artist's eye for form, and would lay an ivy spray by his side, and carve a faithful copy of its graceful outlines; and the design for this, together with an Agnes Dei, to which he had taken a great fancy, formed the decorative terra cotta mouldings round the windows of a model labourer's cottage on his estate, whose erection he used to superintend daily".

THE BRIARY (since largely destroyed by fire, and rebuilt).

G.F.Watts made this his studio - some fine watercolours survive of the view from his window down towards the Bay - and brought here his friends from Little Holland House.

The Prinsep family would often stay here, notably Val Prinsep the painter, whose work includes a portrait of his sister May on High Down; Hallam Tennyson fell in love with it, and years later - after the death of his first wife - married the sitter!

In *More Memories of West Wight*, Eric Toogood includes a photograph of the original house, built in 1873. The Briary was so called because of the profusion of wild roses in the area

Laura Troubridge recalls, from her own childhood, magical summers spent in

"a three storied building in red and white, half villa, half cottage, wholly delightful ... called "The Briary" because of the masses of sweet-briar that grew wild everywhere.

The railway had not come near Freshwater yet, and an exquisite peace brooded over that part of the Island. Nightingales sang in the copse at the back of the Briary.

There were leafy glades formed by tall trees whose branches reached overhead; soft, blustering winds brought the tang of the sea to the garden, which was full of old fashioned flowers, lavender and sweet geranium, and climbing white and yellow roses".

Mrs Watts recounts in "The Annals of a Painter's Life" how

"Signor (G.F.Watts) had been at work at Farringford while Miss (Alice) Liddell and I had spent the morning together under a big elm on the Briary lawn, and when one o'clock came we went to meet the party, as Lord Tennyson and his son had arranged to walk back with Signor.

We had just climbed the little rise that led to a broad green glade when the three came in sight, and we both exclaimed. For down the great aisle of elms there came a white Russian deer-hound flashing like silver through the sun or shade, and the central figure the Poet, a note of black in the midst of the vivid green, grand in the folds of his ample cloak, and his face looming grandly from the shadow of the giant hat. 'Monumental' Signor would have called him.

Tennyson's slight stoop and the heavier step of age, made the youthful figure of his son look all the more what he was, his father's vigorous staff and prop. And then our eyes fell on the delicate grey figure of our beloved Painter on the other side, the grey hat crowning silver hair, a grey cloak taking pleasant folds while he stepped like a boy, light and neat in every movement. Lord Tennyson was playful, gave us a smiling greeting, and put out the crook of his walking stick for us to shake hands with.

As we went towards The Briary the teeming life of nature seemed to turn their thoughts to a life beyond this life. Lord Tennyson quoted with regret the saddest epitaph he knew, written by a friend who had no belief in the future; and then with moistening eyes he gave us the triumphant words placed over a woman's grave: 'I have loved, I love, I shall love.' But given in the terse Latin, 'Amavi, Amo, Amabo.'"

GLENHEADON

Agnes Weld:

"A little side gate led from the Briary garden into "Love Lane" which is just like a Devonshire lane in miniature, and leads into a succession of fields, along which Tennyson used to walk to Glen Headon, so called from that bit of the Highlands of Scotland, transplanted, as it were, to the Isle of Wight which was named Headon Hill, and at whose foot Glen Headon lay overlooking Totland Bay.

Here dwelt the father and mother of the well known judge Lord Bowen; Mr Bowen used to interest my father immensely by the many thrilling episodes he had to tell of scenes in his clerical life which began in a curacy among wild Irish folk.

Despite his great age, Mr Bowen used to perform the service most impressively at the Totland Church which he was the means of having erected".

Glenheadon is opposite Christ Church, Totland Bay, built in 1875 at the Revd Bowen's instigation; the house is approached via York Lane.

The original wooden church was re-erected on Totland beach as a library and reading room. Recently restored, it is now a restaurant.

WESTON MANOR

Squire Ward, a close friend of Tennyson, had Weston Manor built when he had to resign holy orders because of his conversion to Catholicism. Mrs Cameron would load a donkey cart with photographic equipment and come up here to work; the results, if outdoor shots, do not appear to survive. Agnes Weld recalls that

"from the field at the south side of Hawkridge to Weston Manor House, on the opposite hill, wound a special gravel path, made for his own use by the squire of Weston Manor, Mr W.G.Ward, known to a generation as "The Ideal Ward", because of his book on "The Ideal of a Christian Church" which caused him the loss of his fellowship at Oxford.

He was at one time President of the Metaphysical Society, of which Tennyson was a member, and in whose formation Professor Pritchard had a share, and both men were equally ardent students of philosophy, and had in common a perfectly guileless child-like nature.

The mixture of the dreamy student and the hearty friend in Mr Ward was very amusing, for his carriage had generally half passed by before he discovered that a lady had bowed to him, and then he would spring up, as if shot, turn right round, and bow effusively, hat in hand".

In the Gazetteer for this period, W.G.Ward's other address is given as Northwood House, Cowes, his grandfather's old home.

Wilfred Ward recalls his father was Tennyson's neighbour from 1870 to 1882, though he visited the West Wight frequently in the 1860s, and was introduced to the poet by Dean Bradley. For the younger Ward,

"Freshwater was in those days seething with intellectual life. The Poet was, of course, its centre, and that remarkable woman Mrs Cameron, was stage-manager for what was for us young people a great drama.

Speaking generally, it was a society in which good breeding, literary taste, general information and personal distinction counted for much more than worldly or official status. Genius was all in all for us - officialdom and conventionality in general were unpopular in Freshwater"

The Chapel at Weston Manor was replaced as the main place of worship in 1923 with the building of St Saviour's Roman Catholic Church.

In the Catholic graveyard across the road, the Ward family tomb, topped by a large statue of Christ crucified. This forms the setting for a crucial scene in D.H.Lawrence's early novel "The Trespasser", set in and around the Bay.

The graveyard also contains the tomb of the poet Alfred Noyes - author of "The Highwayman" - who lived on the Undercliff.

THE HAWKRIDGE

As its name suggests, this occupies a commanding position near the stone windmill - since demolished - at the top of Windmill Lane, off Summers Lane. Here lived Mrs Agnes Weld, niece of the poet and author of a fine book of reminiscences of the Freshwater set.

Agnes Weld later recalled,

"Just before we left our home, I was informed that during the whole of the fifteen years we had occupied Hawkridge, its grounds had been used as a hiding place for illicit spirits.

This explained the noises which had awakened and puzzled me in the dead of night - the long drawn out whistle which was the signal for the shuffling of feet and the rolling of a heavy body along the ground, followed at one time by a runaway ring at the front door, at another by the tramp of hobnailed boots across our cellar"

HURST HILL

Now the Youth Hostel; Tennyson would take the field path next to the Briary to walk across the fields to Hurst Hill.

Agnes Weld recalls how *"The road that led from Farringford to the Pritchards' house passed at the foot of the hill on which Hawkridge, our own house, was built."*

Charles Pritchard was one of Tennyson's intimate friends, a clergyman who later became Professor of Astronomy at Oxford. Agnes Weld: *"Well do I remember his bringing his microscope to Farringford, and showing my uncle some recent deep-sea dredgings by polarised light".*

Hallam's Memoir records Tennyson visiting Pritchard

"to look thro' his telescope, and was charmed with the nebula in Hercules, "that mighty firmament"; and with Jupiter and his four moons "filling all the field"

Pritchard's widow remembered that *"the view from his library windows, overlooking the Solent and Hurst Castle, was his special delight".*

ALL SAINTS, FRESHWATER

Overlooking the Causeway. Built in the 11th Century; with a major Victorian restoration in 1875.

There are memorials to Tennyson - who worshipped here - and his family inside the church. In the South aisle is a stained glass window - designed by Watts - for which Emily Tennyson, as an angel, and Ellen Terry, as a very feminine Sir Galahad, were the models.

Emily Tennyson and Mary Hillier are buried in the All Saints churchyard. There is also a substantial family vault. There is a touching Latin memorial to Lionel, the poet's son buried at sea, set in the wall - next to a similar memorial to the poet himself.

The base of a statue to St John, to the right of the High Altar, also commemorates Lionel.

The church clock chimes were composed by Sir John Stainer, and are known as the Tennyson chimes.

As Hester Fuller records,

"It is the honour and glory of Freshwater that on the tablet put up to his memory in our beautiful old church is the following inscription:

In loving memory
of
Alfred Lord Tennyson.
Whose happiest days were passed at Farringford in
this Parish.

Born August 6th, 1809
Died October 6th, 1892
Buried in Westminster Abbey
October 12th 1892"

MEMORIAL HALL, FRESHWATER

The new Drill Hall was erected in 1899 for the Artillery Volunteers, reputedly as a memorial to Mrs Cameron, who had subscribed £100 to its appeal. The foundation stone was laid by Hallam Tennyson, and the building was opened by Sir Charles Seeley.

In the early 1960s the building was bought by Freshwater and Totland Parish Councils, and converted into the Memorial Hall for community use. In the council chamber upstairs is a fine collection of Cameron photographs, in modern reproduction.

BELLE VIEW

Near the railway station. Home, after Alfred's death, to his brother Arthur, who also was marked by a *"cloaked figure and striking face"*, and could almost have been the poet's ghost.

HEATHFIELD HOUSE

Holiday residence of Granville Bradley, Dean of Westminster. His children played with Tennyson's two sons, while, as Bradley's daughter recalled,

"the two men roamed the country together, poetising, botanising, geologising. I can see my father now, a slight, active little figure, armed with a hammer and girt with a capacious knapsack, setting forth joyous as a chamois-hunter, for a day's sport among the fossils of the Isle of Wight cliffs".

It was Bradley who brought down his brother-in-law, the music scholar Sir George Grove, for the first of his many visits to Farringford, and he in turn brought his close friend, Sir Arthur Sullivan.

LYMINGTON

William Allingham, when not visiting Farringford, was Customs House Officer here.

Through his good offices, Mr Sellwood - Emily Tennyson's aged father - moved to Aubrey House, at Keyhaven. From here, semaphone signals were exchanged across the Solent between this house and Farringford.

Tennyson's brother Charles Tennyson Turner, the sonneteer - a man who escaped severe opium addiction to become a priest in the Church of England - wrote of the Island viewed from here.

THE NEEDLES LIGHT HOUSE
From Audrey House, Keyhaven

The Downs and tender tinted cliffs are lost
And nothing but the guardian fire remains,
That crimson-headed tower on the rough coast
Whose steady lustre flashes not nor wanes
Til sunrise from the east restores again
The mighty Vectian wold and tawny tract
Of shingle seen through bowers of arbutus
Like some fair cornfield mellow and compact.
How that deep glow the deepending gloom attests,
How much is by that high-set lighthouse taught.
Mine eye rests on it as the spirit rests
In sorrow on some holy ardent thought,
The sole light in our darkness! Those who dwell
Near these great beacons are instructed well.

This is a fine elegy, too, on the great days of Tennyson and his friends, as immortalised through the lens of Mrs Cameron.

EDEN HOUSE, TOTLAND

Summer residence of Violet Hammersley. A close friend of the Bloomsbury set, she was awarded their supreme accolade, to be painted by Duncan Grant.

At Eden House, she played host to prominent literary figures like Aldous Huxley, Rosamund Lehmann - who spent part of the 2nd World War here - and Christopher Isherwood.

ALUM BAY

William Allingham records a walk in December 1863;

"A.T., Palgrave and I walk to Alum Bay and look at the coloured cliffs, smeary in effect, like something spilt".

Four years later, Allingham and Tennyson walk near Alum Bay, *"he thinks 'England is going down' - 'Christianity becoming extinct. There's something miraculous in man'. 'There's more in Christianity than people think'.*

MAP OF FRESHWATER BAY

The Bay
1. Glenbrook
2. Fort Redoubt
3. Plumley's Hotel
   (now the Holiday Fellowship)

Coastguard Lane
4. Ocean View

Gate Lane
5. Albion Hotel
6. Beach House
7. Baker's Farm
8. Stark's Hotel
9. The Mall
10. St. Agnes Church
11. Orchard's Store

Victoria Road
12. Whitecliff House
13. Monksfield
14. Holly Tree Cottage
15. Myrtle Cottage

The Square
16. Hazlehurst
17. Havelock
18. The Porch *(since demolished)*

Terrace Lane
19. Terrace House
20. The Pannells
21. Redoubt House
22. Dimbola Lodge
    (now Dimbola/Cameron House)

Bedbury Lane
23. Farringford Hous
24. Roseberry Lodge
25. Farringford Lodge
26. Farringford Farm

27. High Down
    (now Tennyson Down)
28. Watcombe Bay

Moon's Hill
29. Middleton Farm Cottages
30. The Briary *(since rebuilt)*

Glenheadon
Weston Manor
The Hawkridge
Hurst Hill
Memorial Hall
Heathfield House
Eden House
} *not shown on map*

Map (from Isle of Wight Guide Map) reproduced by kind permission of Service Publications Ltd., Shoreham-by-Sea, Sussex

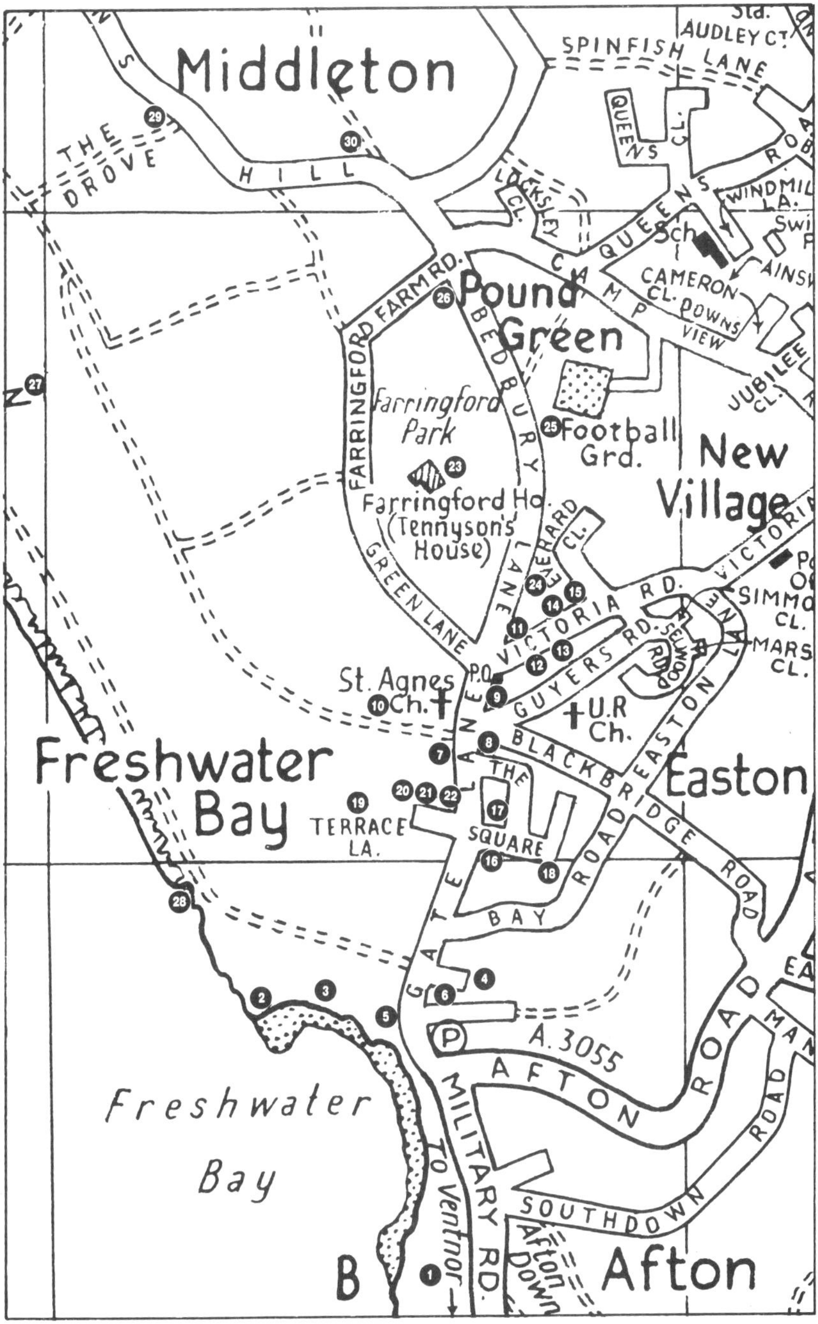
Middleton
Pound Green
New Village
Freshwater Bay
Easton
Afton
Freshwater Bay
Farringford Park
Farringford Ho. (Tennyson's House)
Football Grd.
St. Agnes Ch.
U.R Ch.
P.O.
Sch
THE DROVE
HILL
SPINFISH LANE
AUDLEY CT.
QUEENS CL.
QUEENS RD.
WINDMILL LA.
LOCKSLEY CL.
CAMP RD.
CAMERON CL.
DOWNS VIEW
JUBILEE CL.
FARRINGFORD FARM RD.
BEDBURY LANE
GREEN LANE
EVERARD CL.
VICTORIA RD.
GUYERS RD.
SELWOOD RD.
SIMMONS CL.
MARSH CL.
EASTON LANE
BLACKBRIDGE ROAD
THE SQUARE
TERRACE LA.
GATE LANE
BAY ROAD
A.3055
AFTON ROAD
MILITARY RD.
SOUTHDOWN ROAD
Afton Down
To Ventnor
B

Snapshots: Contemporary Views of Julia Margaret Cameron

Extracts from Contemporary Journals

1860

June 14th: I hear a tramping on the drive when I am resting after dinner and think that it is Americans coming as seven did the other day to ask for admittance but find that it is Mrs Cameron's Grand piano which she has most kindly sent for Mr Lear.

It is pleasant to see the surprise of each one coming in & seeing it. The Camerons in the evening. Mr Lear sings a long time. ET

1862

July 1st: Mrs Cameron comes across the Park looking gorgeous in her violet dress & red cloak walking over the newly mown grass. Pleasant to hear the men cheering. ET

1863

December 26th: At Yarmouth I find Mrs Cameron shopping, who gives me a seat in her carriage, and tells me she has a copy of Henry Taylor's Works for me as a Christmas Box.

In a subsequent examination which she puts me through as to my opinion of HT's poetry I fear my answering fell decidedly below her expectation, for the Christmas box was never given, nor did either of us mention it afterwards. WA

1864

October 8th: Crossed to Yarmouth in the steamer. Mrs Cameron on board and Anthony Trollope and wife. I sat next Anthony outside the coach to Freshwater; he asked a great many practical questions about the houses and lands which we drove past - did not seem interested about Tennyson. WA

1865

Easter: Mrs Cameron sits up till two o'clock in the morning over her soaking photographs.

I cannot tell you how much we enjoy it all; of a morning the sun comes blazing so cheerfully, and the sea sparkles, and there is a far-away hill all green, and a cottage which takes one's breath it looks so pretty in the morning mists. Then come eggs and bacon. Then we go to the down top. Then we lunch off eggs and bacon. Then we have tea and look out of the window, then we pay little visits, then we dine off eggs and bacon, and of an evening Minny and Emmy robed in picturesque Indian shawls, sit by the fire, and Miss Stephen and I stroll about in the moonlight.

Mr Prinsep wears a long veil and a high coned hat and quantities of coats. It is so heavenly lilac down here. There are nothing but poets and painters everywhere, and it is so gold and delicious up over the downs.

I am quite sure about Mrs Cameron's photographs. She paddles in cold water till two o'clock every morning. Mrs Cameron says, "Why does not Mrs Smith come to be *photographed.* I hear she is *Beautiful.* Bid her come, and she shall be made *Immortal*". AT

June 24th: Farringford; hid my bag - find some people in the hay-field and Mrs Cameron photographing everybody like mad.

Went to house. Alfred Tennyson says "*Are you come to stay?*" I confess the bag, and we go to fetch it. Mrs Cameron focuses me, but it proves a failure, and I decline further operations. She thinks it a great honour to be done by her. WA

November 1st: Custom House, pay pensioners. William Barnes has been invited to go with me to Farringford, and we cross to Yarmouth, nearly fouling a collier on the way.

Tea: enter Mrs Cameron (in a funny red open-work shawl) with two of her boys. T reappears, and Mrs C shows a small firework toy called 'Pharaoh's Serpents',a kind of pastile, which when lighted, twists about in a worm-like shape. Mrs C said they were poisonous and forbade us all to touch. T in defiance put out his hand.

'*Don't touch 'em!*' shrieked Mrs C. '*You sha'n't, Alfred!*' But Alfred did. '*Wash your hands then!*' But Alfred wouldn't, and rubbed his moustache instead, enjoying Mrs C's agonies. Then she said to him: '*Will you come tomorrow and be photographed?*' He, very emphatically, '*No*'.

T and I went out to the porch with Mrs C, where her donkey chaise was waiting in the moonlight. WA

1866

October 16th: Mrs Cameron & Lady Manners join us in the evening when Mr Sullivan sings his '*Oh Mistress Mine*' and '*Sweet Day*'. ET

October 26th: Mrs Cameron brings a variegated laurel. Generous creature, how hard it is to stay her hands from gifts! ET

1867

September 16th: Have several pressing notes from Mrs Cameron to come and bring Dante Gabriel Rossetti to her - '*photograph you both*'. I ask him will he come today. Decidedly, '*No!*' WA

September 17th: I try to get Rossetti over to the Island, and coax him as far as the pier, but it is rather windy,and he entirely objects to be sea-sick, and doesn't want to see either Mrs Cameron or Tennyson. WA

November 25th: Mrs Cameron brings a photograph of Horatio. He looks in it like one of Landseer's Stags, not one of the 'King's Sons'. ET

1868

June 8th: In the evening Mr Palgrave *(editor of famous Anthology)* performs the Muslem service & the summons to prayer. Very solemn and imposing. ET

June 9th: Mrs Cameron photographs him. All go to croquet at Norton. ET

June 20th: Coach to Freshwater. Mrs Cameron's; long wait for lunch. Mrs C. and her household take no note of time. Meet girls going upstairs in fancy dresses. Mrs C has been photographing a group, and appears carrying glass negative in her collodonised hands. *'Magnificent! to focus them all in one picture, such an effort'.* WA

September 1st: Mrs Cameron opens her wooden room with a ball. We let Lionel go for a little while. The room overflows so much that many are alfresco under the beautiful moon. ET

October 17th: A.T. and I down the lane; call at Miss Thackeray's where they are at luncheon; then at Mrs Cameron's. He says, as we approach her house: *'Mrs C.(using the initial, as he often does) is so gushing!'*

She presently justifies this by saying fervently to T., while we spoke of F.Walker, '*His soul is at your feet!*' Says T., '*I hope his soles are at his own feet*'.

We go to the shore with the Ritchies. T. throws a stick into the sea for dog to fetch. WA

1869

January 3rd: Rehearsals for the Play at Mrs Cameron's Theatre. ET

January 8th: The theatre now enlarged and ready. The play a triumphant success. Good and generous Mrs Cameron reports that with Mr Jowett's and Mr Henry Taylor's gifts will enable her to found the Hospital she wants to found here. ET

1871

February 17th: Lord Elcho walks with A. and I talk to Lady Elcho of Mrs Cameron's wonderful acts of love & of all the orphans & the desolate creatures she receives under her roof. Surely there was never a larger heart. ET

December 5th: Delightful to see Mrs Cameron at the Station rushing towards one with open arms. ET

ET = Emily Tennyson; WA = William Allingham; AT = Anne Thackeray

Mrs Cameron: Eyewitness Reports

Hester Fuller writes of Mrs Cameron;

"It was here that she lived, ruled, and devoted her life to art, to friendship, and to being kind to everybody. Her dynamic and all-compelling individuality, her unconventionality, and her outspoken frankness were the delight as well as the astonishment of her hosts of friends.

In a book, long since out of print, my mother says: "It is almost impossible to describe Mrs Cameron; she played the game of life with such vivid courage and disregard for ordinary rules: she entered into other people's interests with such warm-hearted sympathy and determined devotion, that though her subjects may have occasionally rebelled, they generally ended by gratefully succumbing to her rule, laughing and protesting all the time".

As Mrs Cameron wrote in "Annals of a Glass House", "I worked fruitlessly, but not hopelessly; I longed to attest all the beauty that came across my way".

Mrs Cameron worked in the days when art in connection with the camera had never been thought of. She brought all her genius and energy to the development of her ideas. Anyone who has ever seen a "Daguerreotype" will realises the revolution Mrs Cameron created by her photographs. She held frequent exhibitions of her work at Colnaghi's Gallery in London. Her portraits of famous people and her pictures of sacred subjects after the manner of the Italian masters revealed to an amazed public the possibilities of the camera. She gained gold, silver, and bronze medals in England, America, Austria and Germany.

I have before me as I write, a book of Mrs Cameron's photographs which she made and gave to my mother. On the dark-green morocco cover is printed, in letters of gold: Given to Annie Thackerary by her friend Julia Margaret Cameron. Freshwater Bay, Isle of Wight.

On opening the album the first thing one sees is the following caution, written by Mrs Cameron in her big, bold handwriting: "Fatal to photographs are cups of tea and coffee, candles and lamps, and children's fingers!".

"Indeed", writes my mother, "Mrs Cameron followed her art with extraordinary trouble and devotion, and also expected much from her sitters. Sitting to her was a serious affair, not to be lightly entered upon. Her sitters came at her summons, they trembled, or would have trembled, could they have dared, when the round black eye of the camera was turned upon them. They felt what consequences, what disastrous waste of time and money and effort might ensue from any passing quiver of emotion". For in those days Mrs Cameron had to make her own plates, and her sitters would have to sit without moving for ten minutes while the cap was off the lens".

This was the time when Mrs Cameron was illustrating Tennyson's "Idylls of the King" and many sitters were needed, and I have heard descriptions of all the dressing up that was needed and of "strangely robed men and maidens issuing forth from the Glass House" where the photographs were taken.

Mr Wilfred Ward has written: "Freshwater in these days seethed with intellectual life. The Poet, was, of course, the centre, and that remarkable woman, Mrs Cameron, was stage manager of what was, for us young people, a great drama. For Tennyson was still writing the "Idylls of the King" which had so greatly moved the whole country, and we felt that we were in the making of history".

Tradition in Freshwater still tells of all the kindness and help given by Mrs Cameron to people in trouble, and how all were made welcome to her house. I have heard my mother describe how her garden gate was never shut and how brown paper parcels were spread out on the lawn, as well as open pans of collodium which were used for developing the photographs. From my mother's descriptions I seem still to hear the echo of Mrs Cameron's voice calling to her maids, and the voice of the master of the house reciting Homer aloud in the drawing-room. Tennyson's description of him was "a philosopher with his beard dipped in moonlight".

A friend has told me how she was taken by Mrs Cameron into Mr Cameron's bedroom where he lay fast asleep on his bed. Mrs Cameron, pointing to him, said: "Behold the most beautiful old man on earth". I recall the story of when Garibaldi came to Farringford to see Tennyson. Mrs Cameron went down on her knees before him to implore him to sit for his photograph. Garibaldi did not understand this, and thought she was a beggar asking for alms.

Of a dinner party for Alfred Tennyson, Sir Henry Taylor, my mother, and the Misses Prinsep, at Dimbola, Mrs Cameron writes: "We dined at seven and only got up from the table at eleven o'clock. All the while the most brilliant conversation. The whole range of poetry, comprising every immortal poet brought to life and living again in the glowing wise breath of Alfred Tennyson and the quotations from Henry Taylor's rich and faithful memory..... They were like two brilliant fencers crossing their rapier or flashing their foils, both giving and evading clean thrusts".

Agnes Weld thought highly of her uncle's *"dearest woman friend ... who seemed to be all the famous women of the French salons of the 18th Century rolled into one, with an added charm of her own besides"*. This echoes Wilfred Ward's summation of the Freshwater circle. For Mrs Weld, Julia

"was a woman of earnest piety and rare intellectual powers, and especially was she the very incarnation of friendship; no trouble was ever too great for her to take or serve or give pleasure to the many she folded to her motherly heart, and when with Mrs Cameron she made each feel that he or she was the only being in the whole universe for whom the Queen of Friends lived.

This rare power was only attained by an utter and exhausting sacrifice of self - a sacrifice which, while it undoubtedly shortened Mrs Cameron's life, made it infinitely better worth living.

However busy she might be, she would put it aside if a friend came to her for advice in difficulty, or congratulation in joy, or solace in sorrow. A boundless enthusiasm and an unquenchable optimism enabled her to see and seize upon the best side of peope and force them to act up to it, and influence the world for good to a degree of which they had not hitherto thought themselves capable.

She refused to be bound by any of the artificialities of modern society life, and her complete freedom from affectation was a great refreshment to Tennyson, and even made him bear patiently the many scoldings she gave him for refusing to waste (as he considered it) the precious hours of lovely summer mornings in sitting to her for his photograph.

Concerning Mrs Cameron's generosity, all of her friends were quite afraid of ever admiring anything belonging to her, for the moment they did so she insisted on making a present of it them there and then."

Yet to a child, Julia could be a strange, frightening figure. Laura Gurney, one of her young models, recalled her as *"a strange wilful creature, and a law to herself"*. In her autobiography, *Memories and Reflections*, Laura declares that

"To me, I frankly own, she appeared as a terrifying elderly woman, short and squat, with none of the Pattle grace and beauty about her, though more than her fair share of their

passionate energy and wilfulness. Dressed in dark clothes, stained with chemicals from the photography (and smelling of them too), with a plump, eager face and piercing eyes and a voice husky, and a little harsh, yet in some way compelling and even charming, my first sight of her was in her studio at Dimbola, the little cottage home at Freshwater, about a quarter of a mile from the sea; and immediately we, Rachel and I, were pressed into the service of the camera. Our roles were no less than those of two of the angels of the Nativity, and to sustain them we were scantily clad, and each had a pair of heavy swan's wings fastened to her narrow shoulders , while Aunt Julia, with ungentle hand, touzled our hair to get rid of its prim nursery look.

No wonder those old photographs of us, leaning over imaginary ramparts of heaven, look anxious and wistful. This is how we felt, for we never knew what Aunt Julia was going to do next, nor did anyone else for the matter of that. All we were conscious of was that once in her clutches we were perfectly helpless. "Stand there", she shouted. And we stood there for hours, if necessary, gazing at the model of the Heavenly Babe (in reality a sleeping child deposited in a property manger). The parents, anxious and uneasy, were outside, no more able to rescue their infant until Aunt Julia had finished with it, than we should have been.

Aunt Julia photographed every one she met, great people and small ones. No tourist was safe. Men and women gazing quietly at the sea or walking down the dusty lanes that zigzagged between flowering hedges, were liable to find themselves bidden in a way that brooked no denial into her studio, where, a few moments later, they would find themselves posing as Geraint, or Enid, Launcelot, or Guinever, or any other legendary hero or heroine; and they would learn more about their own faces than the looking-glass had ever told them, for Mrs Cameron had the real artist's faculty of piercing through the outward structure to the very soul of the individual.

. *No-one had ever undertaken a real portrait study until Aunt Julia with her hobby and her unconventionality, revolutionised all previous ideas upon the subject by producing, though in a rough and ready state, what in reality were works of art. How well I remember those profile and three-quarter heads of Madonnas and other fair, mystical looking women."*

The ordeal of posing for Mrs Cameron is remembered by a "*lady amateur*" in the pages of the *Photographic News* of 1886;

"The studio was very untidy and very uncomfortable. The exposure began.

A minute went over and I felt as if I must scream; another minute, and the sensation was as if my eyes were coming out of my head; a third, and the back of my neck appeared to be afflicted with palsy; a fourth, and the crown, which was too large began to slip down my forehead; a fifth - but here I utterly broke down, for Mr Cameron, who was very aged, and had unconquerable fits of hilarity which always came in the wrong places, began to laugh audibly, and this was too much for my self-possession, and I was obliged to join the dear old gentleman."

Sir Henry Cotton, who married Mary Ryan, considered that

"After a daring fashion of her own she forfeited the sharpness of outline which ordinary photographers strive for, by placing her sitter far out of focus and subjecting the plate to an unusually long exposure; but the secret of her genius, the study of pose and feature and artistic arrangement of drapery and subject, has not been transmitted to her imitators or successors".

Mary Watts recalls that

"She used to say that in her photography a hundred negatives were destroyed before

she achieved one good result; her object being to overcome realism by diminishing just in the least degree the precision of the focus.

Thus she was able to give her work a poetry and a mystery far removed from the ordinary photographer. While other photographs, after long acquaintance, weary the eye, hers remain an abiding pleasure."

Edith Ellison, one of Dean Bradley's daughters, gives a child's eye view.

"Mrs Cameron was neither mysterious nor awe-inspiring, but just a kind,, exacting though benevolent, tyrant. Children loved her but fled from her. I can see her now, clad in the never-failing wrapper, stained - as were her hands and eager face - with the chemicals she used in her work, her hair falling any way but the right way, lying in wait some fine morning at her garden gate for the young ones passing down the road on their way to Farringford or to the sands of Freshwater Bay.

"She's coming! She'll catch one of us!"

And sure enough an arm would intercept the passage of some luckless wight, and, bribed by jars of preserve or other toothsome dainty, the victim was led away to spend the sunny hours posing in the studio. Photography was then, at the best, a slow and tiresome process, and Mrs Cameron never hurried in her work. Endless were the poses, especially if, as was often the case, the chosen victim was to represent some character in poem or story. Mrs Cameron did not, as a rule, care for mere beauty - she wanted an artistic subject".

Julia Margaret Cameron Album Presented to Nellie Mundy

The original album is held by the Cultural Services Department of the Isle of Wight County Council.

The catalogue card for this volume reveals some information since lost, in rebinding, and is about 25 years old, presumably written at the same time as the Nellie Mundy album was accessioned.

It reads as follows:

"779 CAM Cameron, Julia Margaret, *photographer, Freshwater*
(Album of photographs - portraits. 18-?)

Note on inner front cover "Nellie Mundy with much love from Julia Margaret Cameron. May 23d".

Note on front *e.p.* "All these photographs are from the *life* reduced from the large photographs taken by Mrs Cameron".

Photographs include Tennyson, Henry Taylor, Carlyle, May Prinsep, Lionel Tennyson, C.H.Cameron etc."

The photographs are contained in a bound green folder - into which at some point they have been collated, as some of the accompanying text is cropped - and consist of small, reduced size originals, along with brief notes beneath in Julia Margaret Cameron's own handwriting.

The original dedication to Nellie Mundy, signed by Julia Margaret Cameron, was separated from the album when it was rebound. It has now been rediscovered - thanks to the publicity surrounding plans for this current volume - at Yelfs the binders, and subsequently reunited with the original album!

According to the photographic historian Harry Lunn, Mrs Cameron made fewer than a dozen of these small albums, some of which have since been broken up for sale.

The identity of Nelly Mundy was the subject of a recent entry in the *Times* Diary. With the help of Hugh Noyes and Island genealogist Malcolm Pinhorn, it has been established that she was born Elizabeth Susan Young, daughter of John Young, of Westridge, near Ryde.

In 1838, she married Charles Mundy, a friend of Tennyson, who lived at Ormsby Hall, Lincolnshire. A letter is extant from Alfred to Elizabeth, dated October 1849 and written from Skegness, containing a *grateful recollection* of a recent visit by the poet.

To move from historical fact to conjecture, Elizabeth Mundy may well have first persuaded Tennyson to the charms of her native Isle of Wight.

ALFRED TENNYSON DCL

Alfred, Lord Tennyson (1809-1892) was appointed Poet Laureate in 1850, in succession to Wordsworth.

After Cameron's death, the Autotype Company sold carbon copies of some of her more popular photographs, including this one. Cameron's last major photographic commission was a series of images to accompany the poet's *Idylls of the King*.

In a letter to Henry Taylor, dated Ist July 1876, Cameron wrote "*I wish you would paint a Van Dyke (in words) of Alfred Tennyson. It has been complained of that contemporaries of Shakespeare and Milton did them no justice. Let not the same be said of Alfred Tennyson*".

G.F.Watts wrote to Cameron on much the same lines, about her proposed photographic portrait - "*Do justice to that noble and beautiful head, the finest you will have before your lens*".

Thomas Carlyle described Tennyson as "*one of the finest looking men in the world. A great shock of rough, dusky, dark hair; bright, laughing hazel eyes; massive, aquiline face, most massive yet most delicate*".

Julia once told the poet, "*Although I bully you, I have a corner of worship for you in my heart*".

However, Lady Tennyson considered Cameron's work "*majestic, but lacking delicacy*". She attempted to influence painters and photographers of her husband to tidy up their subject, and give him more nobility.

Tennyson's niece, Agnes Weld, recalls how Mrs Cameron's

"*complete freedom from affectation was a great refreshment to Tennyson, and even made him bear patiently the many scoldings she gave him for refusing to waste (as he considered) the precious hours of lovely summer mornings in sitting to her for his photograph.*

Unfortunately for my uncle, she had discovered what an immense source of pleasure to her friends her photographs of him were ... greatly enhanced when the said photographs were signed with the poet's own autograph.

The more he signed, the more she wanted him to sign; and I have really pitied my uncle when she has come flying up to Farringford with such a huge sheaf of her photographs of him that she has had to hire a carriage to bring them ... with a selection of new pens, so that he might not have the excuse of not having a pen handy to sign them with".

Nevertheless, Agnes Weld also revealed that Julia was "*his dearest woman friend; almost the only woman outside his relations whom he called by her Christian name, and who called him in turn by his*".

Tennyson even had the idea of visiting the Camerons in Ceylon after they had moved back, a scheme firmly scotched by Lady Emily.

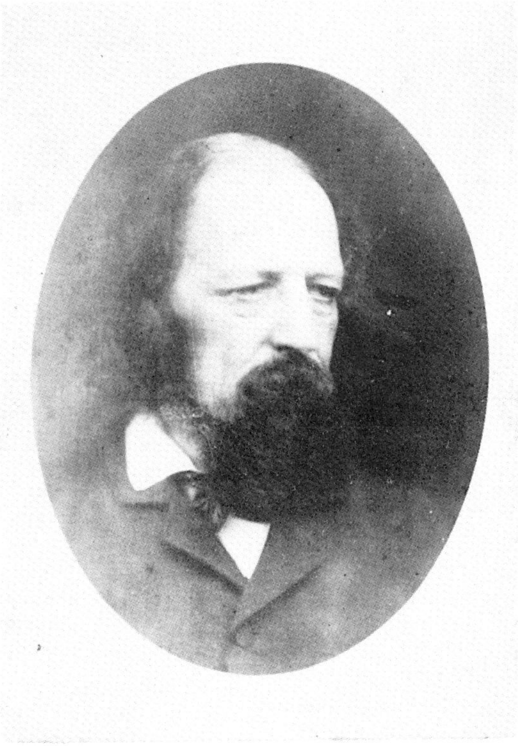

HENRY TAYLOR DCL

Henry Taylor (1800-86) had been one of Tennyson's rivals as Poet Laureate, and another devotee of the Little Holland House set. He published his first poetic drama, "Isaac Commenus" in 1827 and his best known work, the drama in blank verse "Philip van Artevelde" seven years later (a box office failure, but a critical success)

Julia took upon herself the cause of promoting the play, sending review copies to Matthew Arnold and Robert Browning, who tactfully refrained from textual comment. She even issued invitations to a domestic reading, brusquely declined by, among others, John Stewart Mill. After attending the lengthy evening, Holman Hunt remarked that it took as long to sit through her good works as it did for one of her photographs.

Taylor was a civil servant, an important official at the Colonial Office, of which he turned down the under-secretaryship, as he considered his poems to be of greater importance, a view that posterity has yet to echo.

Charles Cameron had known Taylor since both were young men, but Julia met him first in 1848, when she and her husband moved to Ephraim Common, Tunbridge Wells, to be near him. Taylor and his wife would stay at Dimbola Lodge for a week or two each spring, on the way to their summer home at Bournemouth. Cameron would photograph him almost daily, and there are more portraits of him than of any other male sitter.

Julia experimented in her use of highlighting, pulling a calico blind over the wall or roof of her greenhouse to diffuse a white light that would better catch the planes of his face, and the dappled shades of his hair and beard. Indeed, Taylor himself suggested that she refer to his beard as "*The Flower of Love Lies Blanching*".

As early as 1865, Cameron sent off to Scotland, for exhibition, "*a head of Henry Taylor, with the light illuminating the countenance in a way that cannot be described*".

She later wrote that

"our friend ... lent himself greatly to my early efforts. Regardless of the possible dread that sitting to my fancy might be making a fool of himself, he, with greatness which belongs to unselfish affection, consented to be in turn Friar Lawrence with Juliet, Prospero with Miranda, Ahaseurus with Queen Esther. To hold my poker as his sceptre, and do whatever I desired of him. With this great good friend was it true that so utterly

'The chord of self with trembling
Passed with music out of sight'"

Tennyson, perhaps jealous of the admiration he attracted from the photographer, both as model and poet, opined that "*he has a smile like a fish*".

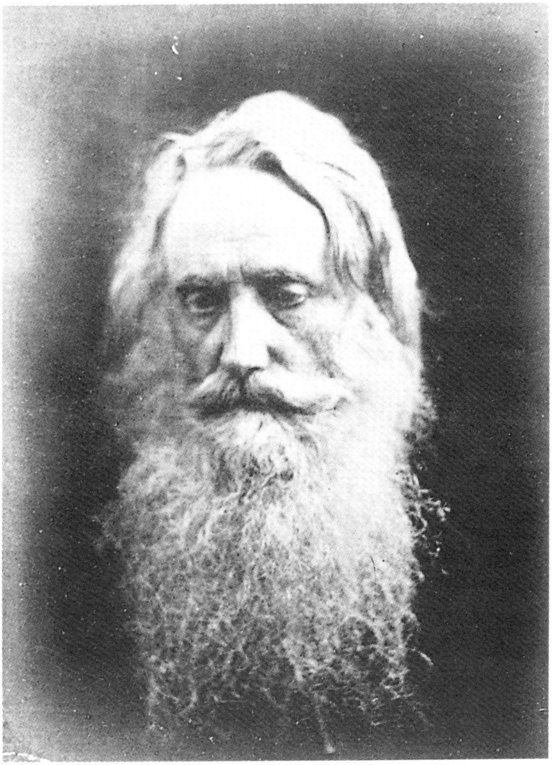

THOMAS CARLYLE

Thomas Carlyle (1795-1881) was a close friend of Henry Taylor and Julia Cameron, and a Trustee of the National Portrait Gallery. On leaving Edinburgh University, he wrote a *Life of Schiller* and, in 1837, *The French Revolution, A History*, which made him the most celebrated literary figure, and lecturer of the age.

After the death of his wife Jane in 1866, he published little. She herself was a great enthusiast for this latest craze.

"Blessed be the inventor of photography. I set him above even the inventor of chloroform. It has given more positive pleasure to poor suffering humanity than anything that has cast up in my time ... I have often gone up to my room in the devil's own humour ... and my eyes, resting, by chance on one of my photographs of long ago places or people, a crowd of gentle thought has rushed into my heart, driven the devil out as clean as ever so much holy water and priestly exorcism could have done"

Indeed, Carlyle was a popular subject for photographic "*cartes-de-visite*". This portrait was taken at Little Holland House, as Julia later recalled, "*to which place I had moved my camera for the sake of taking the great Carlyle*".

When she and Watts visited Carlyle's Chelsea home, Mrs Carlyle relates how Julia was "*hardly to be restrained from forcing her way into Mr C's bedroom while he was changing his trousers. I told her it is a dangerous affair that you are there entering on, Ma'am*"

Henry Taylor remarked jovially that Carlyle's grizzled appearance here might be entitled "*Wormwood Scrubs*".

Carlyle himself wrote to Mrs Cameron that "*it is as if suddenly the picture began to speak, terrifically ugly and woe-begun, but has something of a likeness: my candid opinion*".

The "*sage of Chelsea*" was also photographed full face by Cameron, entitled "*Carlyle like a rough block of Michael Angelo's sculpture*".

Cameron's photographic portraits predate Watts' painting of Carlyle, versions of which can be seen in the V and A, and the National Portrait Gallery. Watts worked in almost as much secrecy as was necessarily imposed by Mrs Cameron's photographic method; screens hid the easel from view, the windows were curtained and the sitter was denied any glimpse of his portrait until it was complete.

Carlyle was as blunt as he had been to Julia. A friend recorded his stern rejoinder phonetically; "*Mon, I'd have ye know that I am in the hobit of wurin' clean lunen*".

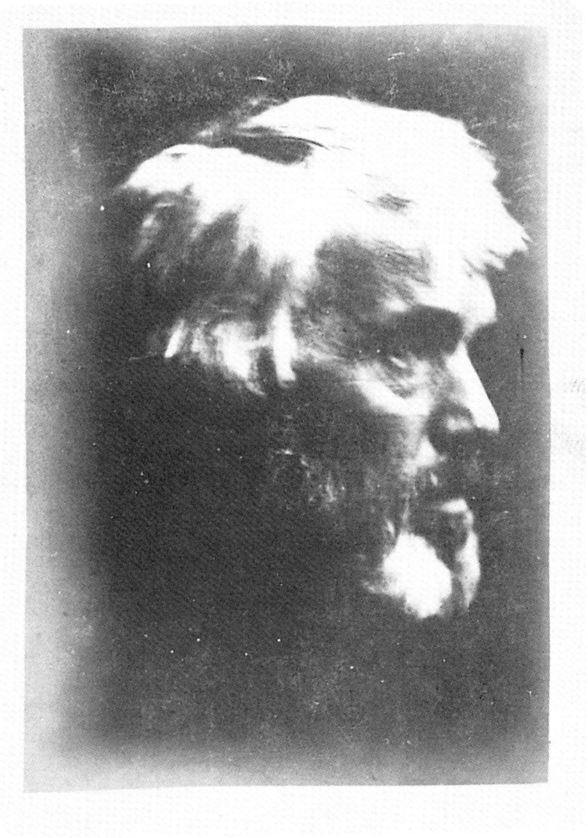

G.F. WATTS R.A.

George Frederick Watts (1817-1904) was trained at the Royal Academy, where he first exhibited at the tender age of 20. He acquired a wealthy Greek patron, Constantine Ionides.

After living with Lord and Lady Holland in Florence as painter-in-residence, he returned to London and there met the Camerons at the salon of her younger sister Sarah Prinsep.

On the return to London of Lord Holland, he was granted an empty "*farmhouse*" on their land, Little Holland House, to which he moved in 1851, along with the Prinseps. "*He came to stay three days, he stayed thirty years*", Sarah recorded.

Watts here painted the three Pattle sisters; Sarah Prinsep, Virginia Lady Somers and Julia Cameron, "*Dash*", "*Beauty*" and "*Talent*".

George Du Maurier wrote of Little Holland House that Watts "*who is universally known as 'The Signor' is their painter in ordinary; the best part of the house has been turned into his studio, and he he lives there, and is worshipped til his manliness has almost departed, I should fancy*".

Cameron joined in this worship; she attached to one of her own photographs a letter from Watts, folded and attached to show the following,as if it were some treasure - "*I beg you to give my love to everybody and believe me to remain yours, GF Watts Signor*".

Many of Cameron's photographs owe their inspiration to Watts' paintings, in their subject matter, their use of (sometimes heavy handed) allegory, the way sitters are posed and dressed in a consciously "*beautiful*" manner, their softness of focus.

He in turn was consciously her mentor in things artistic. Indeed, several of Julia's photographs are inscribed by Watts (including "The Dream"); when she could not cajole him into doing this, she was not above forging his signature.

Watts appreciated the work of his disciple, in another letter he wrote "*I can well appreciate what is noblest in your art, and your last photographs harmonise well with the effect I wish to produce*". On the mount of one photograph, a portrait of Florence Fisher, he inscribed "*I wish that I could have painted such a picture of this*".

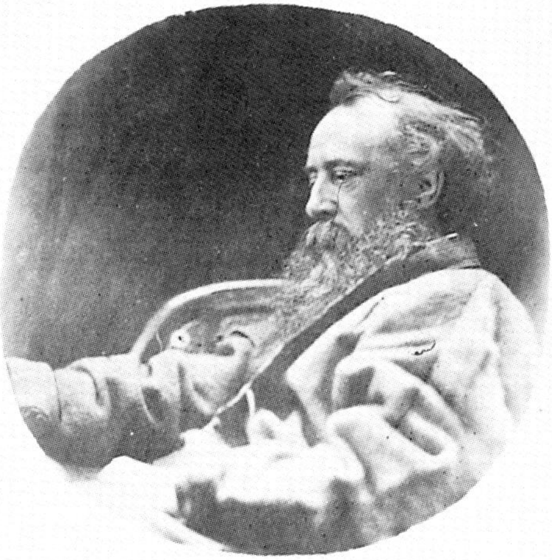

G.F. WATTS R.A.

Watts was a frequent visitor to Freshwater. In 1864 he brought his child bride, the actress Ellen Terry - he was 47, she not quite 17 - who found more satisfaction playing with Tennyson's two children than joining with the adults. In her Memoirs, she happily recalls conversations with Tennyson himself, who treated her in an avuncular manner.

"In the evenings I went walking with Tennyson over the fields, and he would point out to me the differences in the flight of different birds, and tell me to watch their solid phalanxes turning against the sunset, the compact wedge narrowing sharply to a thin line. He taught me to recognise the barks of trees and to call wild flowers by their names. Always I was most at ease with him. He was so wonderfully simple".

Ellen is the subject of one of Mrs Cameron's most magical photographs. The marriage, arranged by "*Pattledom*" for the presumed benefit of the painter, was probably unconsummated, and within a year the couple had separated.

Following the refusal of Lord Holland in 1871 to extend the lease on Little Holland House, Watts supported his old benefactors Sara and Thoby Prinsep by having the Briary built for them, in Freshwater.

Adjoining Tennyson's land, and designed by Philip Webb - the architect of the Red House in Upton, residence of William Morris - it incorporated three large studios for Watts' own use, and he financed it by returning to portraiture, a branch of painting to which he was by now disinclined.

Little Holland House itself was soon demolished, but ironically the villas which were built on its site, still graced by green lawns and shaded groves, themselves attracted a new generation of successful artists - Frederic Leighton, Marcus Stone, Holman Hunt.

Though the Briary was later destroyed by fire, some fine paintings by Watts are still in existence, recording the view fromhis studio looking down towards the Bay.

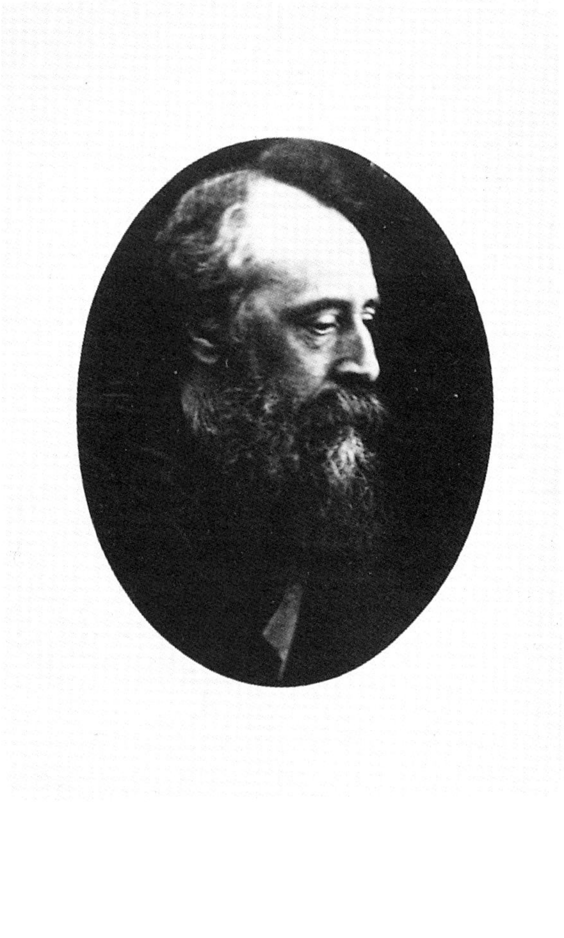

SIR JOHN HERSCHEL

Sir John Herschel (1792-1871) was the son of Sir William Herschel, the great astronomer, and was himself a scientist of genius. Almost as a sideline, Sir John helped pioneer the new science of photography. It was Herschel who discovered how hyposulphite of soda "*dissolves muriate of silver as easily as water dissolves sugar*" - and with a camera obscura he took the world's first photograph on glass.

Herschel kept Cameron, still in India, informed about the progress of photography, and sent her a sample of guncotton, the chemical essence of the wet collodion process with which all her own photographs were taken. Julia noted her gratitude in *Annals of My Glass House*.

"Herschel was to me as a teacher and high priest. From my earliest girlhood I had loved and honoured him, and it was after a friendship of 31 years duration that the high task of giving his portrait to the nation was allotted to me.

He had corresponded with me when the art was in its first infancy ... I was then residing in Calcutta, and scientific discoveries sent to that then benighted land were water to the parched lips of the starved, to say nothing of the blessing of friendship".

Herschel invented the photographic use of sensitised paper, and indeed coined the terms "*photograph*", "*negative*" and "*snapshot*". He was also a close friend of that other early photographic pioneer, W H Fox Talbot.

It was to Herschel that Mrs Cameron presented one of her most important albums, bought for the nation in 1974 after a major public appeal. This is now in the National Museum of Photography, Film and Television, Bradford.

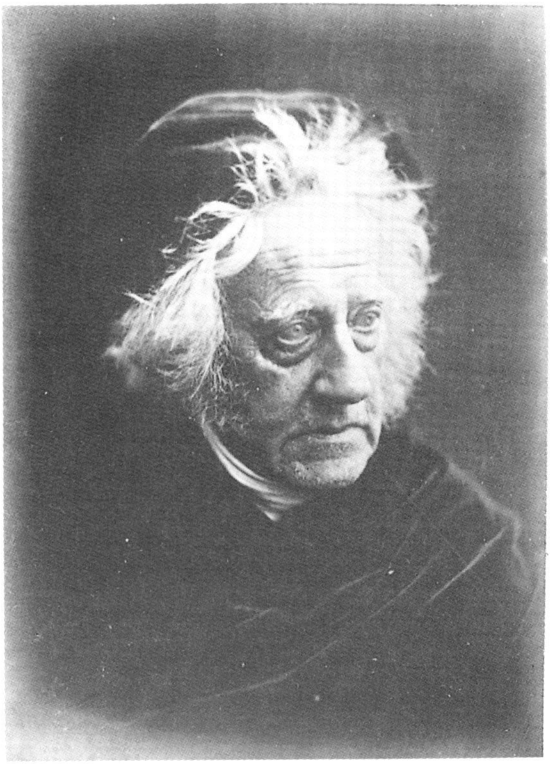

SIR JOHN HERSCHEL

Roger Fry, in his introduction to *Victorian Photographs of Famous Men and Fair Women*, considers that these two studies of Herschel "*seem to me indisputable creations, perfectly distinct*". Indeed, he uses them himself to note a useful distinction in Cameron's work.

"It is curious how much the writers and artists are on show, how anxious they are to keep it up to the required pitch. By comparison, see the supreme unselfconsciousness of the men of science; the Herschel, the Darwin, the Hooker. These men alone possessed an unwavering faith which looked for no external support or approval".

Amanda Hopkinson has described the "*haunted, questing aspect*" of this photograph, its "*inner focus and profound intensity of purpose*". Gernsheim records how, to achieve such profundity, Mrs Cameron made her subject have his hair washed "*to get greater fluffiness in his beautiful mane*".

Sir Henry Taylor, never one to withhold his praise for Julia's work, commented thus.

"It is to my mind one of the greatest triumphs of photography ... that Sir John Herschel's face has been perpetuated, so that future generations as well as the present, may see it in all its grandeur and dignity".

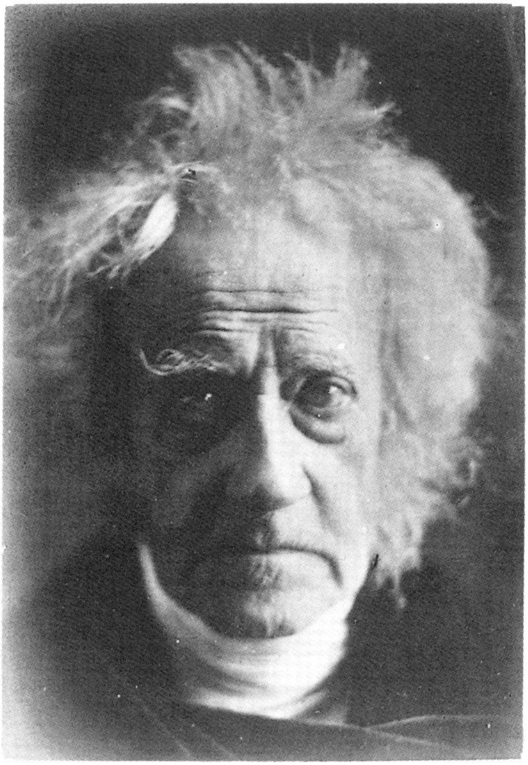

REVD W. BROOKFIELD

The Revd William Henry Brookfield (1809-74) had been a undergraduate with Tennyson at Trinity College, Cambridge, and was to become Queen Victoria's Chaplain-in-Ordinary.

Mrs Cameron once took Anne Ritchie to hear him preach.

"When Mr Brookfield appeared climbing the pulpit stairs to deliver his sermon ... Mrs Cameron chose this moment to lean forwardand kiss her hand to him repeatedly. Poor Mr Brookfield sank down suddenly upon his knees and buried his face in the pulpit cushion".

Tennyson wrote of him with affection after his death.

"Old Brooks, who loved so well to mouth my rhymes
How oft we two have heard St Mary's chimes!
How oft the Cantab supper, host and guest
Would echo helpless laughter to your jest".

Mrs Cameron spent one summer on the Island schooling young Arthur Brookfield, presumably the cleric's son.

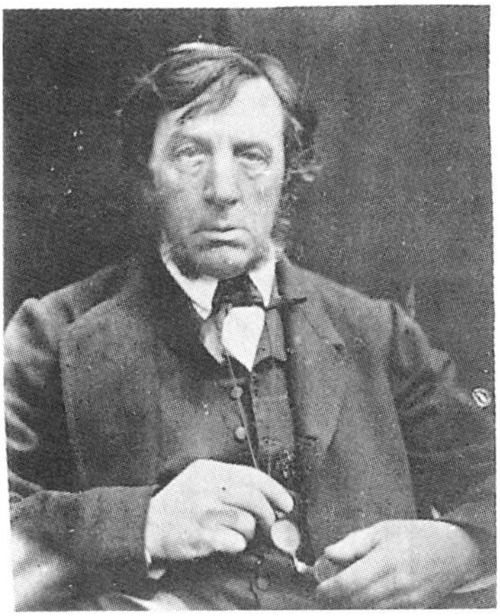

MAY PRINSEP

Mary Emily "May" Prinsep was the daughter of Charles Prinsep, who died in 1864. Her uncle, Henry Thoby Prinsep, was husband to Julia's sister, Sarah, and their residence at Little Holland House was the epicentre of "*Pattledom*".

Of this eccentric household, George Du Maurier uncharitably remarked that it was

"A nest of Proe-Raphelites, where Hunt, Millais, Rossetti, Watts, Leighton etc., Tennyson, the Brownings and Thackeray etc and 'Tutti Quanti' received these women almost kneeling".

It was in such surroundings that May spent her childhood. Left an orphan at the age of thirteen, she was brought up at Little Holland House with her cousins, and often sat as a model for G.F.Watts. She spent several holidays staying with Julia in Dimbola.

May Prinsep's first husband, Andrew Hitchens, died in 1918. The couple had lived near Guildford, and often invited G.F.Watts to visit, having set a studio up for *"the dear little man"*, who later built a house nearby.

She subsequently married Hallam Tennyson, the poet's son and heir.

May was - like Cameron's niece, Julia Jackson - one of Julia's favourite models. Other notable studies include "*May Prinsep, My Princess*", "*Pre-Raphaelite Study*" and "*Beatrice*".

The titles are self explanatory, and capture May's sense of divine stillness, as does another photograph in the present collection, "*The Neapolitan*".

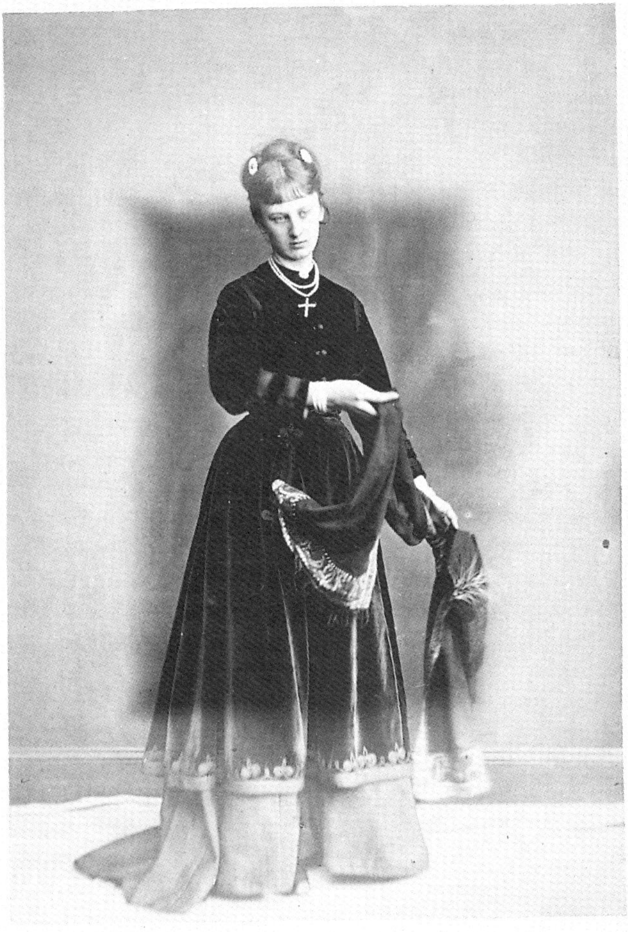

MAY PRINSEP

A painting exists of May standing on High Down, Freshwater, the artist being her cousin, Valentine Cameron Prinsep, the model for "*Taffy*" in George Du Maurier's novel *Trilby.*

Val Prinsep, who lived for a while at the Briary, became a pillar of the Victorian art establishment. He collaborated with Rossetti and Burne-Jones on the Oxford Union murals.

In both these portraits, the stole which May holds in her hands seems to be attached to her dress. As Lady May Tennyson, she is still fondly remembered in the West Wight, as a local benefactor. She was instrumental in setting up a local cottage hospital, a cause begun by Mrs Cameron, for the funds of which amateur theatricals at Dimbola were first instituted.

In her will, May also bequeathed money for an ambulance to be based in Freshwater, for the use of locals. Indeed, a later model is still in daily use - with the distinctive number plate VDL 1 - supplementing the County service, manned by local volunteers, and proudly labelled the "*Tennyson Memorial Ambulance*".

Lady May later moved to the Dower House at Glenbrook St Francis, overlooking the Bay. Here she established a "*clergy library*" of improving books. Her librarian was Allan May, himself an amateur poet of note.

Lady May's will bequeathed a photograph by Mrs Cameron of Emily, Lady Tennyson (now lost) to All Saints church hall.

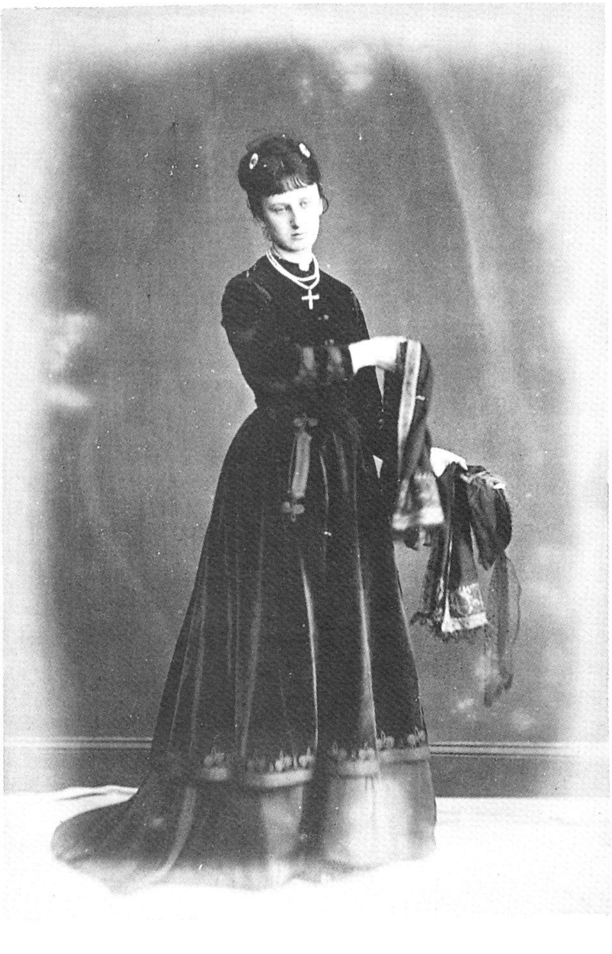

ADRIANA:

Original is life size

The jilted heroine of Jean Boncoeur's novel *Adriana*, serialised and illustrated by Edward Hughes in 1866, is possibly the subject here.

The model is Mary Hillier, a Freshwater girl who became Mrs Cameron's parlour maid, and a frequent photographic victim. There is a sense of mystery which gives an indefinable presence to many of her portraits, notably "*The Dream*".

Nevertheless, Amanda Hopkinson considers that - as Mrs Cameron did all her own developing and printing in Freshwater - Mary Hillier was probably landed with "a *considerable amount of the donkey work*" while her mistress attended to the more exalted duties of "*dressing up and artistic arrangement*".

By some accounts, Mary was known locally as "*Mary Madonna*" - because of her many photographic appearances in that role - and "*Island Mary*", presumably to differentiate her from Mary Ryan.

Of Mary Hillier, Cameron enthused in *Annals of My Glass House*

"*Another little Maid of my own from early girlhood has been one of the most beautiful & constant of my models, -& in every manner of form has her face been reproduced, yet never has it been felt that the grace of the fashion of it has perished. This last Autumn her head illustrating the exquisite Maud*

"There has fallen a splendid tear
From the passion flower at the gate"

Is as pure & perfect in outline as were my Madonna Studies ten years ago, with ten times added pathos in the expression - The very unusual attributes of her character & complexion of her mind if I may so call it, deserve mention in due time, and are the wonder of those whose life is blended with ours as intimate friends of the house".

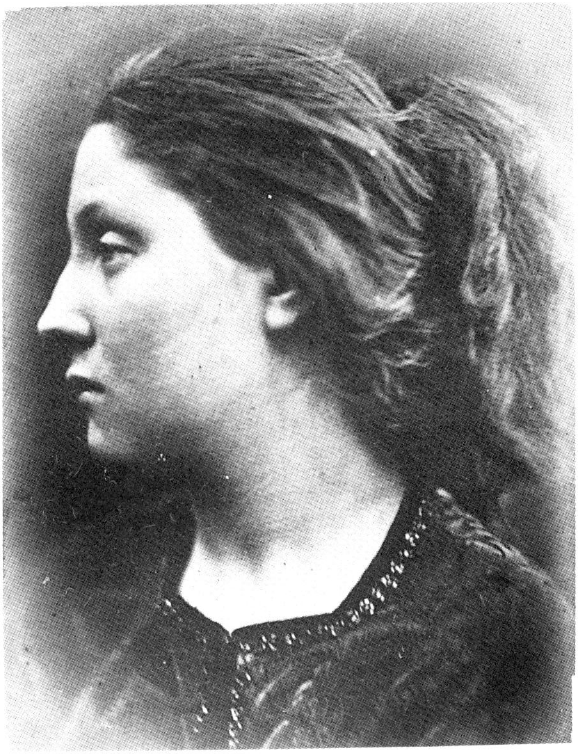

SAPPHO:

Original is life size

Sappho was a Greek poetess who lived in the 6th Century BC; her work expresses passionate feelings towards other women. As Sir William Smith writes in his *Classical Dictionary of Greek and Roman Biography*, published in 1858,

"Modern writers have attempted to prove that the moral character of Sappho was free from all reproach: but it is impossible to read the fragments which remain of her poetry without being forced to come to the conclusion that a female who could write such poetry could not be the pure and virtuous woman, which her modern apologists pretend".

Of the subject, Mary Hillier - Cameron's parlour maid - Amanda Hopkinson relates that "*even in old age and virtually blind, she retained the grace and beauty captured in the photographs of her youth.*"

Mary Hillier was born in Lea Cottage, Pound Green, Freshwater on 19th November 1847, the daughter of a local shoemaker, and had been recommended to the Camerons by her sister Sophia, a maid with the Tennysons. Mary went to work as Mrs Cameron's personal maid in 1861 and remained in their service until they left for Ceylon.

Two years later she married Thomas Gilbert, a railway official, who became G.F.Watts' gardener at the Briary; their eldest child was born in Briary cottage. They had eight children in all, two sons were killed in the Great War - their names appear on the war memorial in Freshwater. Three of her daughters followed her into domestic service.

Colin Ford records that some Freshwater locals still "*remember her as an old lady, allowing schoolchildren to pick apples in her garden for 'a 'apenny a 'atful'*. Mary died in 1936, aged 88, and is buried in All Saints churchyard, close to the Tennyson family vault.. On her tomb is inscribed "*Her children rise up and call her blessed*".

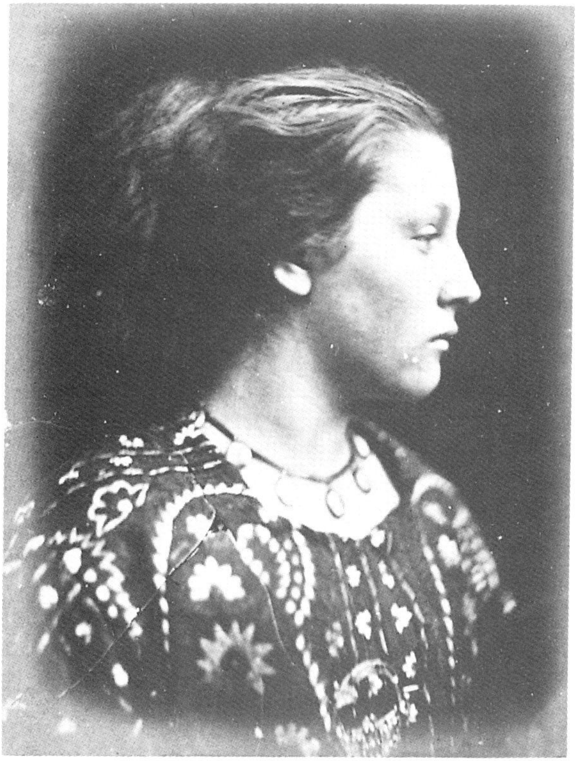

THE NEAPOLITAN

The subject is May Prinsep. Many of Mrs Cameron's ideas came from paintings of the time, and popular taste dwelt on Italian peasants and coloufully dressed young girls.

On the back of one copy of this image, May Prinsep herself has appended a note, dated Advent Sunday, December 1st 1929.

"This framed copy was always in the Poet's Library, and afterwards in Hallam's Study until his death ... chosen by Hallam Tennyson to be the frontispiece to Elaine, Vol VI of the Cabinet Edition of Mr Tennyson's books, 1874. I never knew until after my marriage to Hallam that it had been done. I stayed once for a few months with Mrs Cameron at Dimbola before Mr Watts and the Prinseps lived at the Briary".

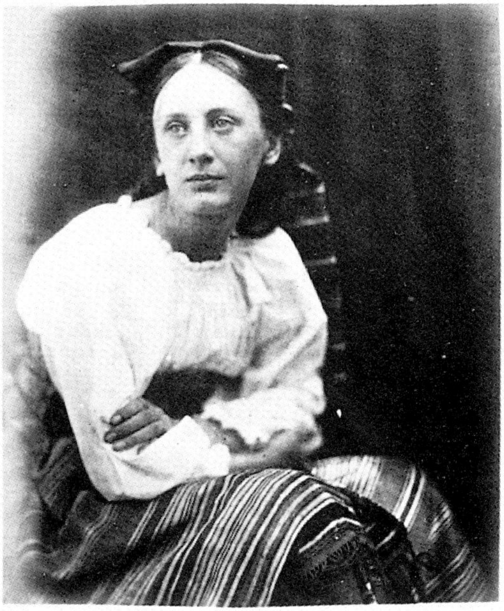

ALICE NO 6;

Original is life size

Alice Du Cane was one of five daughters and three sons of Captain Du Cane of the Royal Engineers. He came to the Island in 1864, shortly after having been appointed Director of Prisons and Inspector-General of Military Prisons, to inspect Parkhurst. As a military engineer, he helped design the chain of forts constructed along the South Coast, following the Crimean War.

"No.6" refers to the fact that this was part of a series of life-sized heads.

Certainly such portraits of young cherubs proved immensely popular, and saleable. Anne Thackeray well describes Julia's photographic stock in trade as being "*Children's solemn eyes and fair waving locks, mothers tending them, Madonnas*".

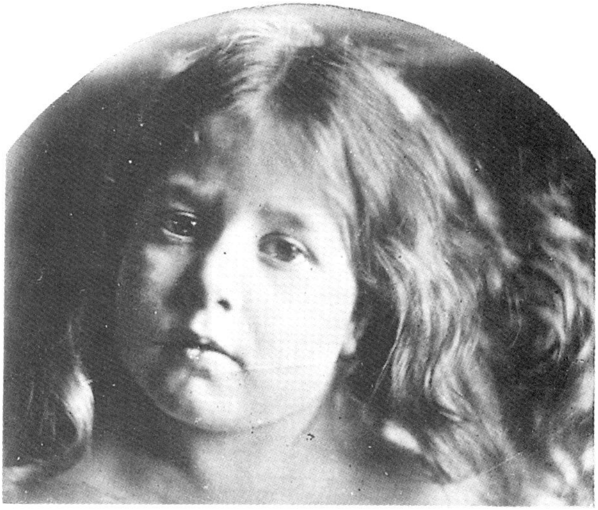

MARY MOTHER

This is from what Julia herself called her "*Raphaelesque Madonna sequence*". As with many of Mrs Cameron's more allegorical treatments, the work is based on an existing painting, here Guido Reni's "*Madonna in Adoration*". As Anna Jameson wrote in *Legends of the Madonna* of 1852,

"*The features are those of a woman in middle age; but in later times the sentiment of beauty predominated over the mother's agony*".

The art critic Roger Fry uses this "*almost complete success*" to point the difference between painter and photographer, when both are imbued with genius.

"*Here the artist has been able to control everything, the mise-en-page, the disposition of the drapery, and the illumination; and the result is almost perfect. No doubt a great painter accepting the data of this would introduce almost unconsciously certain changes.*

The rhythm of the drapery would have been more completely brought out by slight amplifications here and retrenchments there, by a greater variety and consistency of accents, and by certain obliterations.

In particular the awkward direction of the fold seen in the penumbra behind the profile would have been suppressed or changed, and certain curious accidents in the lighted and shaded portions of the lips would have been modified, but none the less few could have surpassed the beauty of modelling of the left-hand side of the face or the exquisite perfection of the contour to the right"

The model for such perfection is again Mary Hillier. Despite the later effusions of Fry, one of the doyens of Bloomsbury, this photograph was entered unsuccessfully at the time for an open competition.

On its prompt rejection, Cameron furiously repudiated the judges competence. Their waspish reply appeared in the *Photographic Journal* of 15 May 1865, mistaking Julia's quest for artistic truth as mere technical incompetence.

"*The Committee much regret that they cannot concur in the lavish praise which has been bestowed on her productions by the non-photographic press, feeling convinced that she will herself adopt an entirely different mode of reproducing her poetic ideas when she has made herself acquainted with the capablilities of her art*".

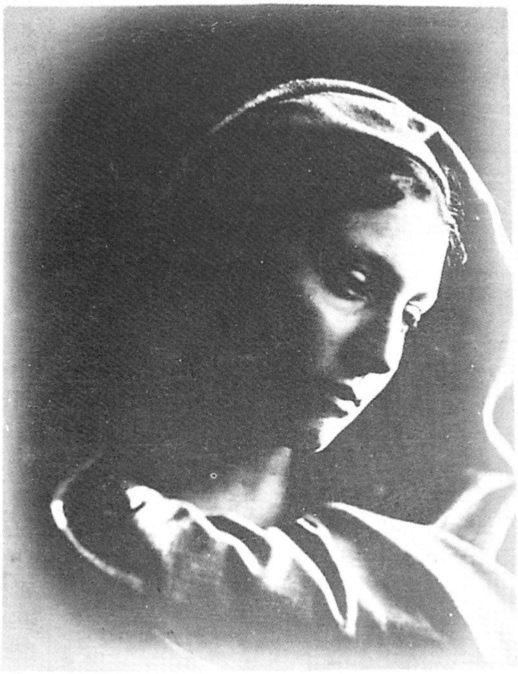

MARY RYAN

When Mrs Cameron was living in Ashburton Cottage, Putney Heath, she was approached by an Irish beggar woman and her daughter, Mary Ryan. With typical impetuosity, Julia offered them one of her cottages, having asked Mrs Ryan's priest to "*give her a character*".

Mary was eventually "adopted" into the family, and moved with the Camerons to the Isle of Wight, where she worked as a parlour maid and photographic model.

Henry Taylor was concerned as to what would become of her;

"If she is to be a servant, I am afraid there is no such thing as a good servant who is fond of reading. If she is to be a governess will she be any happier than governessess who have not been beggars".

He need not have worried. Henry Cotton, a young Indian civil servant had seen her portrait in a London exhibition - as Cordelia, kneeling before King Lear - and immediately fell in love. He worked hard for two years to gain promotion, then wrote to Julia, begging to be allowed to pay court to the young beauty.

Alice Liddell, a frequent visitor to Freshwater, now takes up the story.

"Mrs Cameron at once asked him to stay, and after a time the affair was settled. The wedding ... created no small sensation. The bridegroom brought down a posse of his friends, rather learned, bookish-looking persons. Mrs Cameron, on her part, collected many of the beauties whom her indefatigable energy had hunted up from the neighbouring regions to act as her models".

This was indeed breaking the social taboos. At the eve of wedding dinner, Alice "*sat between two maids and I don't think I ever felt more shy, or had more difficulty in making conversation*".

The wedding took place at All Saints, Freshwater, in 1867. Emily Tennyson records that "*Mr Cameron says he will give her away, but he quakes so at the idea as the day comes near that it is doubtful whether he will find courage when it actually arrives*".

Evidently he did.

Mary, daughter of an Irish tinker, thus eventually became Lady Cotton; the same theme as in Tennyson's poem *The Beggar Maid.*

The marriage was a happy one. Cotton later wrote that Mary

"has since been my devoted companion and helpmate for better and for worse, through many years of vicissitudes and successes, sorrow and aspirations, clouds and sunshine".

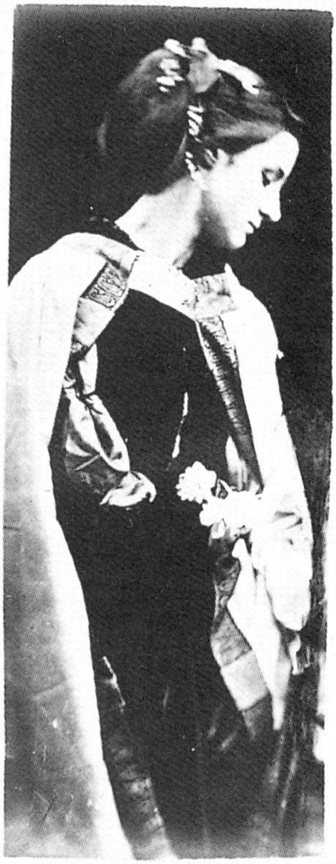

KING DAVID:

Study of HENRY TAYLOR

Taylor would stay with the Camerons in Dimbola each year while his wife Alice went on to open their summer retreat, The Roost, in Bournemouth. In his *Autobiography*, he writes

"I was photographed, I think, almost every day and the photographs being sent to Alice, her opinion was more flattering to them than to me 'I like all except one of the little ones: and most of them I think very grand: decidedly grander than anything you have written or lived; so I expect to think great things of you'".

King David ruled Israel in about 1000 BC. A younger son, who spent his early life as a shepherd, David slew the giant Goliath with a pebble and sling.

He is credited with writing many of the Psalms, and Jewish tradition holds that his descendant will be reborn as the Messiah. The New Testament accentuates his role as a kind of proto-Christ, anointed by Samuel;

Jesus - and divinity is implicit in this photograph - laid great claim to being his direct descendant, and thus heir to the Jewish tradition, the "son of David".

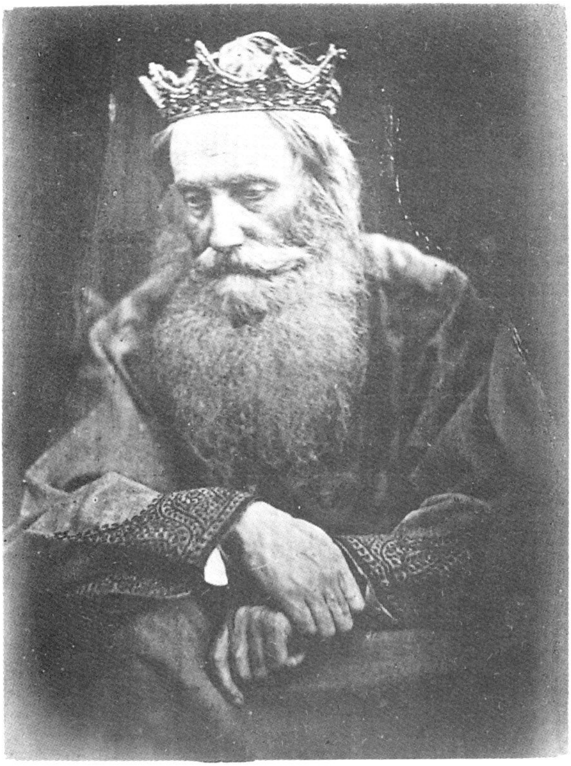

ROSALBA

Original is life size

Princess Rosalba is a character in William Makepeace Thackeray's *Rose and the Ring*, a humorous fairy tale. The more likely context here, however, is Henry Taylor - the poet who Julia championed so largely in vain - and whose poem *Sicilian Summer* has as its heroine a girl of the same name.

> *"In the soft fulness of a rounded grace,*
> *noble of stature, with an inward life*
> *of secret joy sedate, Rosalba stands*
> *as seeing and not knowing she is seen,*
> *like a majestic child, without a want"*.

Jeremy Howard speculates that the model here is Cyllene Wilson's "*more heavily jowled sister*", also adopted by the Camerons. Gernsheim thinks that it is Cyllene herself, who is certainly the model for "*The Mountain Nymph, Sweet Liberty*".

Whowever the model, she appears with a posy of snowdrops and evergreens - possibly myrtle - tucked into the front of her dress as a corsage.

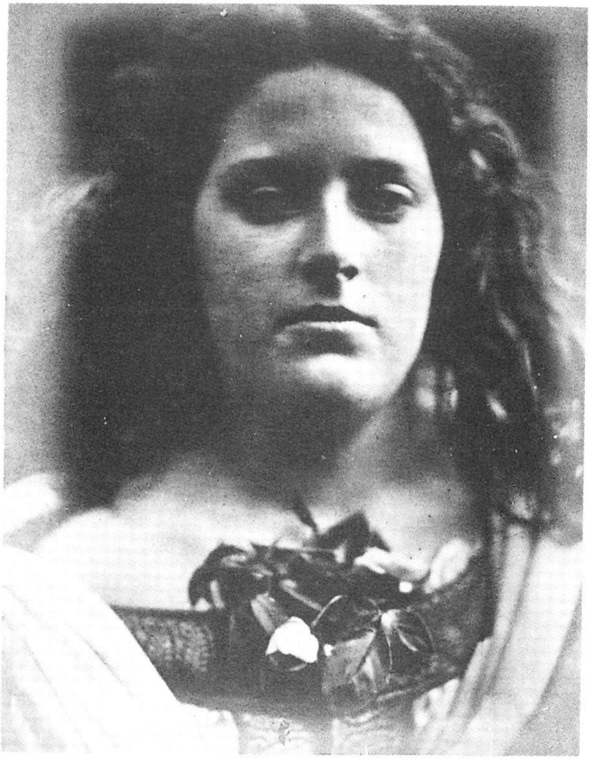

RACHEL

An unidentified model, holding above her head a pitcher of water.

This is a direct reference to the Old Testament. In *Genesis* chapter 29, Jacob meets Rachel, "*beautiful and well favoured*", as she draws water for her father's sheep.

"And it came to pass, when Jacob saw Rachel the daughter of Laban his mother's brother, and the sheep of Laban his mother's brother, that Jacob went near, and rolled the stone from the well's mouth, and watered the flock of Laban his mother's brother.

And Jacob kissed Rachel, and lifted up his voice, and wept."

For seven years, he serves Laban in order to win her hand, but is tricked into marrying her elder sister, Leah. Jacob must work another seven years to gain Rachel as his wife.

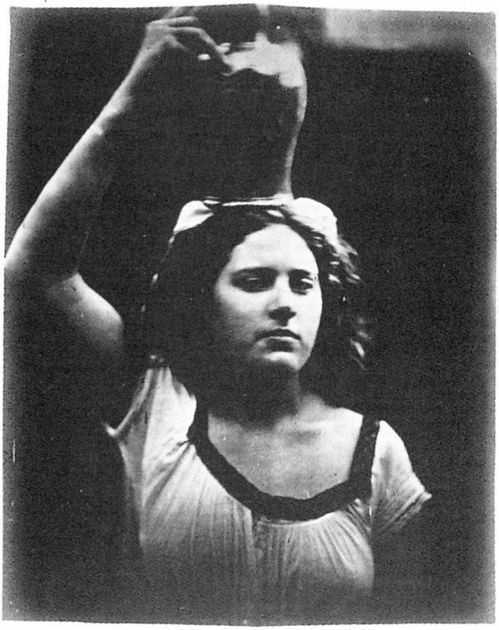

KATE KEOWN

Original is life size

Sister to Elizabeth and Alice Keown. With their baby brother Percy, they appear in a number of guises in Julia Cameron's photographs of the 1860s.

Their father was Thomas Keown, a master gunner in the Royal Artillery, wounded in the Crimea. He was in charge of Fort Redoubt, Freshwater Bay, and all six of his children were born in Freshwater. He left Fort Redoubt in 1870, but a local directory of the following year gives his address as the Royal Standard Hotel, Freshwater.

Of the Keowns, Anne Thackeray Ritchie later wrote "*these were the children who used to come down from the fort with flowers, and who planted Mrs Cameron's banks with primrose roots*".

Elizabeth (nicknamed "Topsy") can be seen in "*Summer Days*", along with May Prinsep and Mary Ryan.

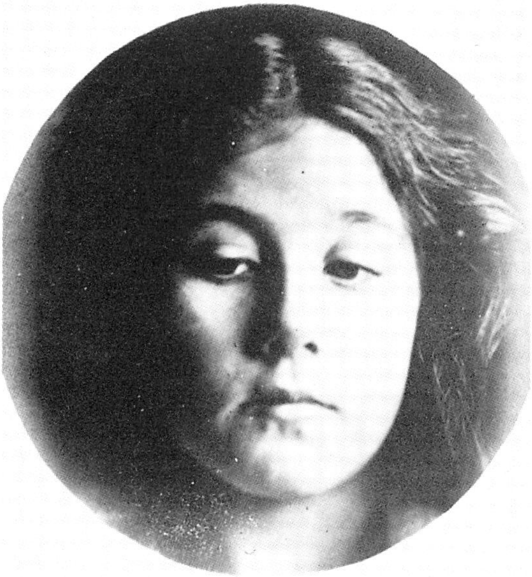

THE BEAUTY OF HOLINESS

This phrase appears four times in the Old Testament, most notably in *Psalms* 29 and 96. In the former, which tradition claims is written by King David, it occurs in the second verse.

"Give unto the LORD, O ye mighty, give unto the LORD glory and strength.

Give unto the LORD the glory due unto his name; worship the LORD in the beauty of holiness".

Psalm 96, "*O Sing unto the LORD a new song*" is abou the coming of the Messiah, and the Judgement at the end of the world.

"O worship the LORD in the beauty of holiness: fear before him, all the earth.

Say among the heathen that the LORD reigneth: the world also shall be established that it shall not be moved: he shall judge the people righteously".

The model here is "Freddie" Gould, one of Cameron's favourite child models, and one who frequently appeared as the infant Jesus, whom both psalms were later seen to prefigure.

William Frederick Gould was born in 1861; his father, also William, was a Freshwater labourer and sailor who lived nearby at Easton.

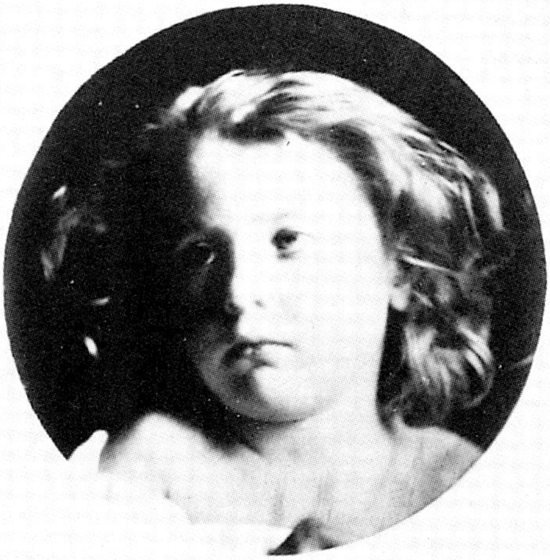

UNCAPTIONED

In the album presented to Henry Taylor, now held at the Bodleian, this has the title "Love in Idleness". In Shakespeare's *A Midsummer Night's Dream*, Act II, Scene I, Oberon, the king of the Fairies, addresses Robin Goodfellow.

"..... I saw, but thou couldst not,
Flying between the cold moon and the earth
Cupid, all armed. A certain aim he took
At a fair vestal throned by the west,
And loosed his love-shaft smartly from his bow
As it should pierce a hundred thousand hearts.
But I might see young Cupid's fiery shaft
Quenched in the chaste beams of the wat'ry moon,
And the imperial vot'ress passed on,
In maiden meditation, fancy-free".

Here is the turning point of the whole play, where Robin - also know as Puck - is despatched to find Cupid's flower, a potion which spreads confusion and lovesickness through the woods of Athens.

"Yet marked I where the bolt of Cupid fell.
It fell upon a little western flower -
Before milk-white; now, purple with love's wound -
And maidens call it love-in-idleness.
Fetch me that flower; the herb I showed thee once.
The juice of it on sleeping eyelids laid
Will make or man or woman madly dote
Upon the next live creature that it sees".

The model for Cupid here, suitably mischievous, is Freddie Gould; there is a hint also of Puck, who vows to "*put a girdle round about the earth/in forty minutes*" to gather this herb.

In the album which Julia presented to Maria Jackson, this photograph is simply entitled "Cupid", which lacks the resonance of the Shakespearean reference.

Cupid was the Roman god of love, son to Mercury and Venus, and identified with the Greek divinity, Eros.

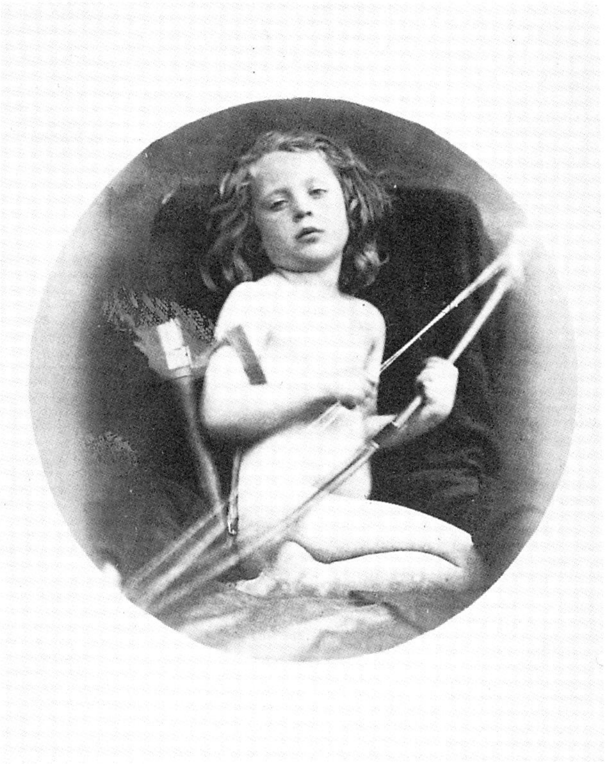

YOUNG ASTYANAX

One of Mrs Cameron's few forays into classical myth. In a brilliant piece of literary detection, Colin Ford points out that this subject probably derives from Sir John Herschel's translation of the *Iliad*, extracts of which appeared in the *Cornhill Magazine*, two years before this photograph was taken, in 1866.

In Greek legend, Prince Scamandrius was the son of the Trojan prince Hector and his wife Andromache, and thus grandson of King Priam.

When Hector is killed by Achilles, the Trojans rename the boy 'Astyanax' (translated as Lord of the City) in honour of his father's bravery. The Greek commander, Agamemmon, decrees that he too must die, in case he becomes a focus for the defeated Trojans. After the fall of Troy, he is thrown from the battlements of the city by the Greek warrior Neoptolemus.

In Euripides' play *The Trojan Women*, his mother bewails this cruel murder of an innocent child.

"Oh darling child, prized at too great a worth to live!
You die, at enemy hands, and leave me desolate,
Your noble father's greatness, which to other men
Brought hope and life and victory, will cost you your death".

However, according to medieval legend, young Astyanax survives to found the kingdom of Messina in Sicily. His most illustrious descendant was the Emperor Charlemagne.

The model here is Freddie Gould.

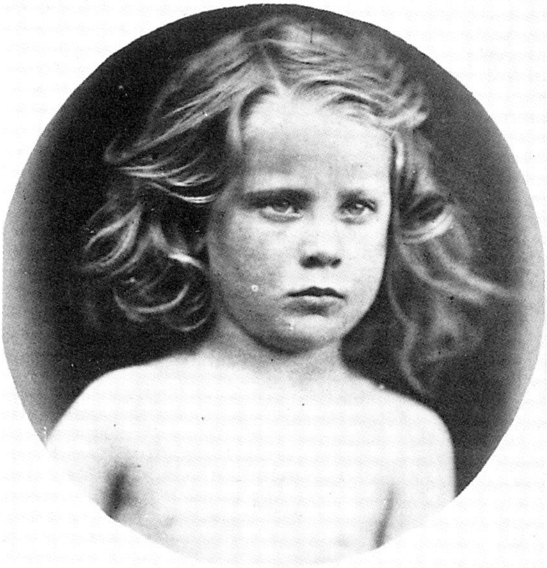

THE MOUNTAIN NYMPH, SWEET LIBERTY

The title is drawn from Milton's poem of 1632, *L'Allegro*, which forms a pair with *Il Penseroso*, matching light and shade, day and night, joy and melancholy.

Here, Milton summons Euphrosyne, goddess of "*Jest and youthful jollity*",

"Come, and trip it as you go
On the light fantastic toe;
and in thy right hand lead with thee
the mountain nymph, sweet Liberty;
And if I give thee honour due
Mirth, admit me of thy crew".

Amanda Hopkinson thinks this photograph "*uniquely mysterious*". Herschel was much of the same mind, though more technical in his praise. In a letter to Mrs Cameron, he wrote:

"That head of the mountain nymph, Sweet Liberty (a little farouche and egaree by the way, as if at first let loose and half afraid that it was too good) is really a most astonishing piece of high relief. She is absolutely alive and thrusting out her head from the paper into the air. This is your own special style."

The model here is Cyllene Wilson (1851-83). Her father, the Revd Samuel Wilson, was a missionary who translated the New Testament into modern Greek. He railed against "*seducers in our age*", for "*if our children have no fixed principle of religion, they become an easy prey*". It is ironic that in her own short life, Cyllene was married three times, and three times divorced!

Cyllene hated being photographed by Julia. No wonder, for to get the right expression for "*Despair*", Mrs Cameron once locked her reluctant model in a closet for two hours.

After the death of her father, Cyllene was "adopted" by the Camerons, but in 1870 she ran away to sea She became a stewardess and married the first engineer on an Atlantic liner. Cyllene died of yellow fever, in Argentina, aged only 33.

Cameron inscribed on another print of this photograph, "*from the once perfect, now damaged negative*".

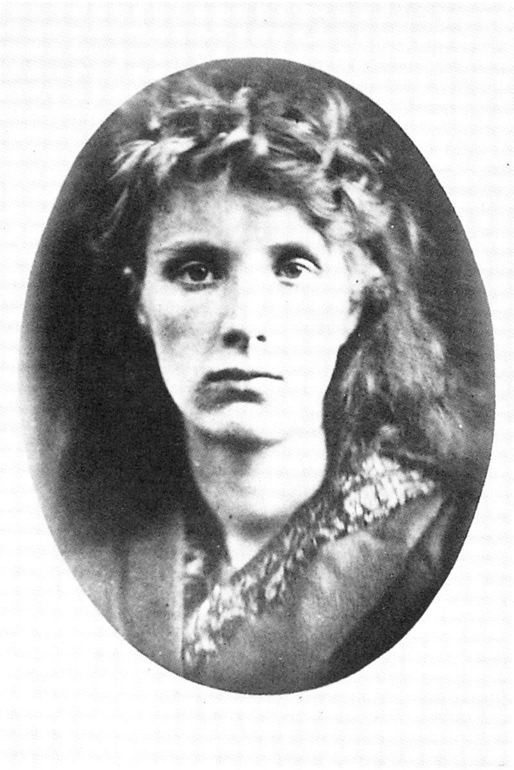

"IF YOU'RE WAKING, CALL ME EARLY, CALL ME EARLY, MOTHER DEAR"

Tennyson's *May Queen*

The models here are Mary Ryan and Caroline Hawkins, of whom little more is known.

Cameron's illustration is for the second part of the poem, "New Year's Eve", in which the once happy heroine realises that this Mayday will be her last!

"If you're waking call me early, call me early, mother dear,
For I would see the sun rise upon the glad New-year.
It is the last new-year that I shall ever see,
Then you may lay me low i' the mould and think no more of me.

To-night I saw the sun set: he set and left behind
The good old year, the dear old time, and all my peace of mind;
And the New-Year's coming up, mother, but I shall never see
The blossom on the blackthorn, the leaf upon the tree ..."

This mournful theme continues for another eleven verses, but Tennyson obviously takes pity on this sense of youth cut short, and the *May Queen* concludes with a temporary reprieve.

"And what is life, that we should moan? why make we such ado?

For ever and for ever, all in a blessed home -
And there to wait a little while till you and Effie come -
To lie within the light of God, as I lie upon your breast -
And the wicked cease from troubling, and the weary are at rest".

The young girl is now better reconciled to her fate.

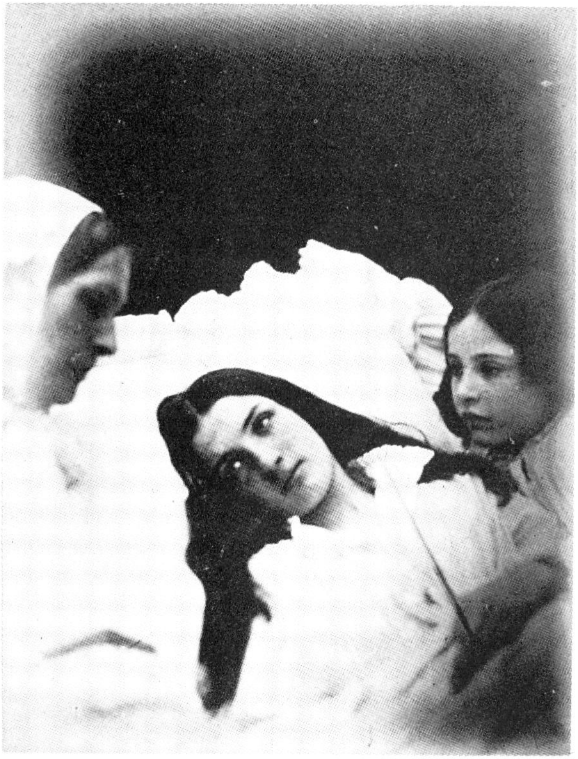

LA MADONNA RIPOSATA: "RESTING IN HOPE"

The models are Mary Hillier and Percy Keown. Colin Ford notes that unlike the Renaissance originals on which such photographs are based, tiny children would not remain still long enough, so infants of three or four had to be used, and she had to pose her Madonnas so that they could hold their children to help them keep still. Yet Anne Thackeray Ritchie found the result effective;

A sweet woman's head, a child safely cradled in her arms, the old tender maternal story retold once more is called "Resting in Hope".

In the front of the photographic album which Julia Cameron presented to Lady Ritchie is a more realistic awareness of the nature of young children; "*Fatal to photographs are cups of tea and coffee, candles and lamps, and children's fingers*"!

The title here is drawn from the "*Riposo*", the Holy Family on their flight into Egypt, either resting or at the close of their journey.

Wilfred Ward later described the indignities poor Mary had to suffer; Mrs Cameron

"would show off to her friends the Mary who was called, from the shape of her face, 'Madonna', using various devices to exhibit her to the best advantage. 'Mary, do stand on that chair and pull down that high curtain'. Then, turning to her friend, 'Isn't she perfect in that light, and in profile as you see her now'".

Cameron was herself to write of Mary Hillier,

"So many think I idealize and glorify my beautiful madonna but I Know all her expressions - and know all the beauty".

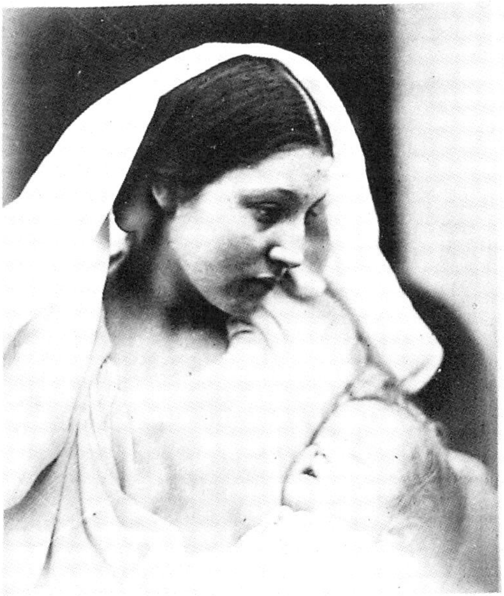

FRIAR LAWRENCE AND JULIET

From Shakespeare's *Romeo and Juliet*, Act IV, Scene I, in which the Friar persuades Juliet to take a sleeping draught.

"Take thou this vial, being then in bed,
And this distilled liquor drink thou off,
When presently through all thy veins shall run
A cold and drowsy humour; for no pulse
Shall keep his native progress ...
And in this borrowed likeness of shrunk death
Thou shalt continue two-and-forty hours,
And then awake as from a pleasant sleep"

An alternative version of this photograph actually depicts the Friar passing over this vial to Juliet. The plan, of course, backfires. Romeo, thinking that Juliet really is dead, takes his own life, as does Juliet herself when she awakes to find him.

The models here are Henry Taylor and Mary Ann Hillier. Henry Taylor later noted his photogenic appeal;

"There is a feature of my life, conspicuous in my photographs, which dates from this period ... this is my beard. In 1859 my hand was so liable to be shaken by asthmatic spasms that the razor was not safe in it, and it was laid by. In the last days of that year I notified in a letter to one of my girl friends the small beginnings of what was soon to be developed into the phenomenon presented by Mrs Cameron's art in multiform impersonations of David, King Lear and all sorts of

'Kings, princes, prelates, potentates and peers'"

Hopkinson indicates how Cameron's work focused on "*the inter-relationship between an elderly, venerable and often powerful 'potentate' ... juxtaposed with a young maiden, often in an attitude of appeal*".

Henry Taylor and Charles Cameron usually took the role of kingship; whereas any available servant would serve for the female! Emily Tennyson complained how, when one of her own maids was pressed into action; "*I sent a housemaid around with coffee. Mrs Cameron returned the coffee, but posed the servant in flowing robes as Goneril*".

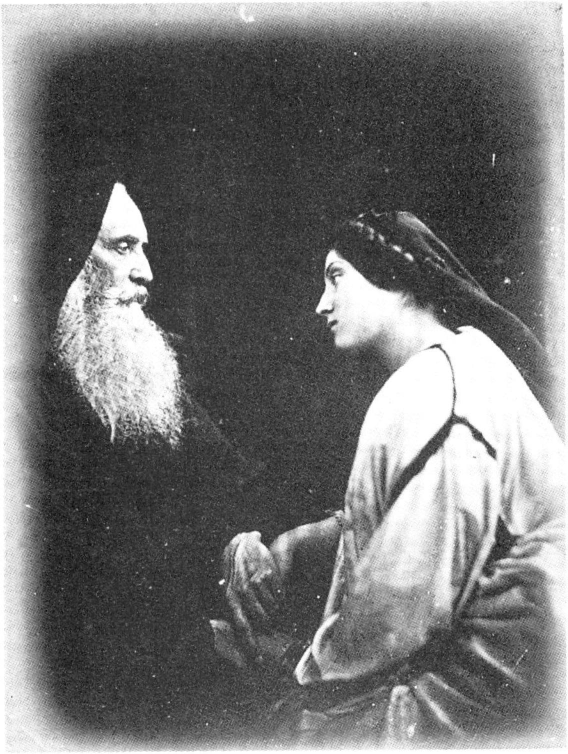

LA MADONNA VIGILANTE: "WATCHING ALWAYS"

Mary Ryan, with white head-dress and gown. The Infant Jesus is possibly Freddie Gould. A companion piece to the "*Madonna Riposata*". Lady Tennyson wrote in a letter to Edward Lear - *not* an admirer of the photographer - that

"Mrs Cameron is making endless Madonnas and May Queens and Foolish Virgins and Wise Virgins and I know not what besides. It really is wonderful how she puts her spirit into people."

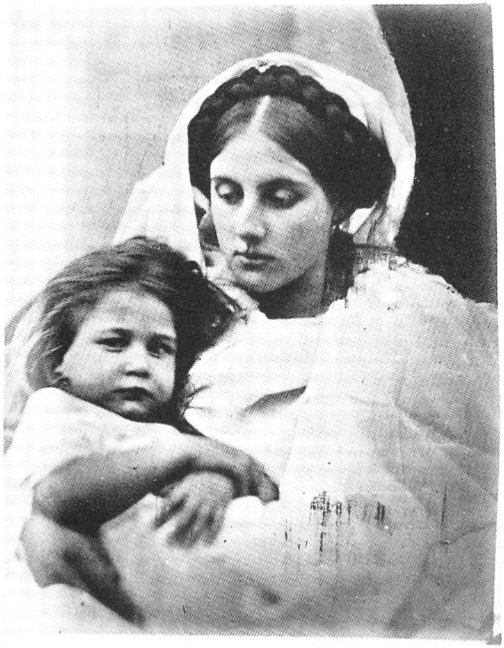

"SEVENTY YEARS AGO MY DARLING, SEVENTY YEARS AGO"

Tennyson's "Grandmother"

The model for the old lady is Sarah Groves, with white bonnet. The model for the young girl is unidentitified. Sarah Groves lived on the Farringford estate. At the age of 94, she was one of Freshwater's oldest inhabitants, and the widow of a master carpenter; she died within a year of this photograph being taken.

The title is drawn from verse 6 of Tennyson's poem, *The Grandmother*, based on a story of Benjamin Jowett, to whom an old woman had once said "*The spirits of my children always seem to hover about me*". Here, the grandmother recalls her own youth.

"For I remember a quarrel I had with your father, my dear,
All for a slanderous story, that cost me many a tear,
I mean your grandfather, Annie: it cost me a world of woe,
Seventy years ago, my darling, seventy years ago".

She speaks, like the May Queen, from her death bed.

"There is but a trifle left you, when I shall have past away.
But stay with the old woman now: you cannot have long to stay".

The poem is addressed to her grand-daughter, Annie. It begins with Annie just having told her of the untimely death of Willy, her "*eldest-born*" son, long estranged, at the tender age of 70.

In *Three Freshwater Friends*, Hester Fuller writes

"An old wrinkled woman and a young child illustrate "Seventy years ago, my darling, seventy years ago" - which reminds me of Mrs Cameron's saying that "No woman should ever allow herself to be photographed between the ages of eighteen and eighty".

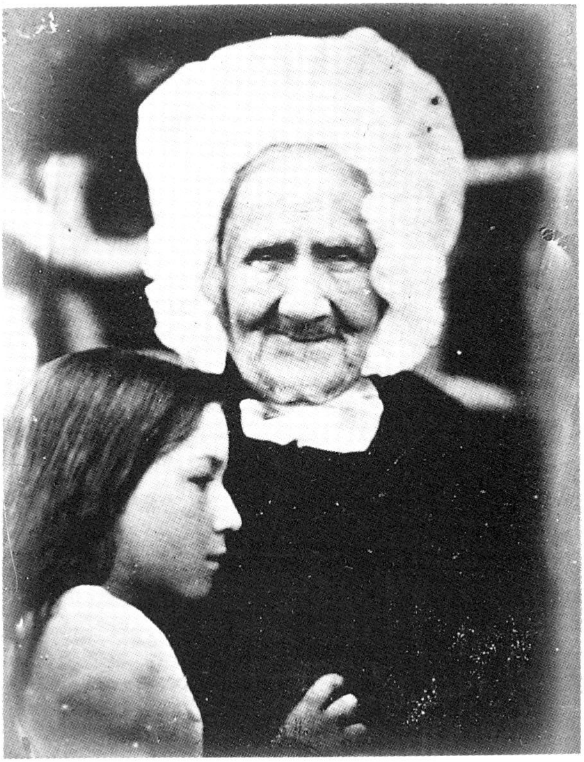

MRS HERBERT DUCKWORTH:

Original is life size

In the Herschel, this is titled "My favourite Picture. My Niece Julia".

Julia Jackson (1846-1895) was the daughter of Julia's sister Maria and Dr John Jackson, who coincidentally had been at school with Tennyson. She turned down proposals of marriage from Holman Hunt and the sculptor Thomas Woolner, who "*worshipped*" her delicate bone structure. Julia's first husband, the barrister Herbert Duckworth, died in 1870; she bore him three children, one of whom - Gerald - went on to form the publishing house of that name.

She subsequently married Leslie Stephen in 1878: G.F.Watts, who painted her, and later Stephen, in oils as a wedding present, commented that "*it was a life that gave strength to one's own by merely knowing that it was there*".

The novelist George Meredith, another of her early admirers, was more blunt, commenting to Vanessa Bell that Stephen "*was the only man in my knowledge worthy of being mated with your mother*".

Leslie Stephen himself was previously married to Harriet Thackeray - sister to Annie - who died suddenly when pregnant. By such coincidences was the path prepared for the "Bloomsbury Group", literally children of the Dimbola/Little Holland House axis.

In 1917, Virginia Woolf, Julia Jackson's daughter, founded the Hogarth Press, and in 1926 paid tribute to her great aunt by publishing 450 copies of *Victorian Photographs of Famous Men and Fair Women by Julia Margaret Cameron*, the first book devoted solely to her work. Virginia includes three portraits of her mother.

Julia Jackson also appears, thinly disguised as Mrs Ramsay, in Woolf's 1927 novel, *To the Lighthouse*. The portrait is unmistakeable, once having seen Mrs Cameron's photographs of Julia: "*The Graces assembling seemed to have joined hands in meadows of Asphodel to compose that face*".

Visual beauty is not, of course, the whole picture. Amanda Hopkinson relates a contemporary account of Julia Jackson, which comes as no surprise to those who have read Virginia Woolf's own private letters and diaries.

"She would say something so unexpected from that Madonna face, one thought it vicious".

To redress the balance, Hester Fuller writes of one of Mrs Cameron's studies of her niece, that it was

"... so beautiful that one feels photography will and never can go further".

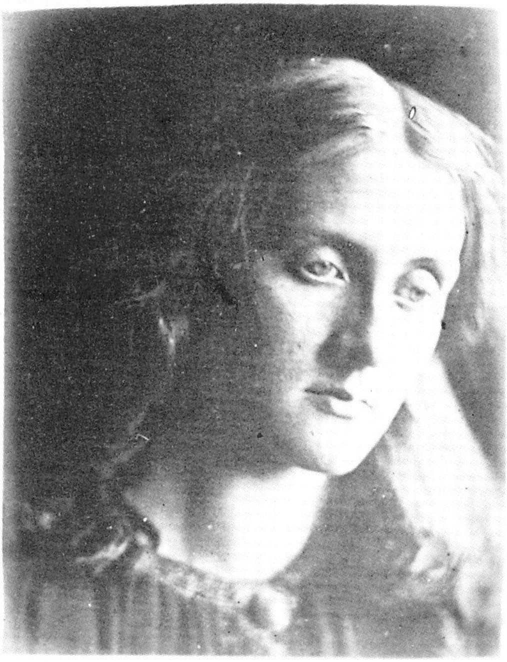

"WE SING A SLOW CONTENTED SONG AND KNOCK AT PARADISE"

Another version of this photograph, entitled either "The Minstrel Group" or "The Wandering Minstrels", has an extra figure on the right. Yet another version contains only the (adult) figure on the left.

In the full version, the three models used are Mary Ryan, Katie Keown and Lizzie Keown (cropped from this version).

The source of the quotation is yet to be identified.

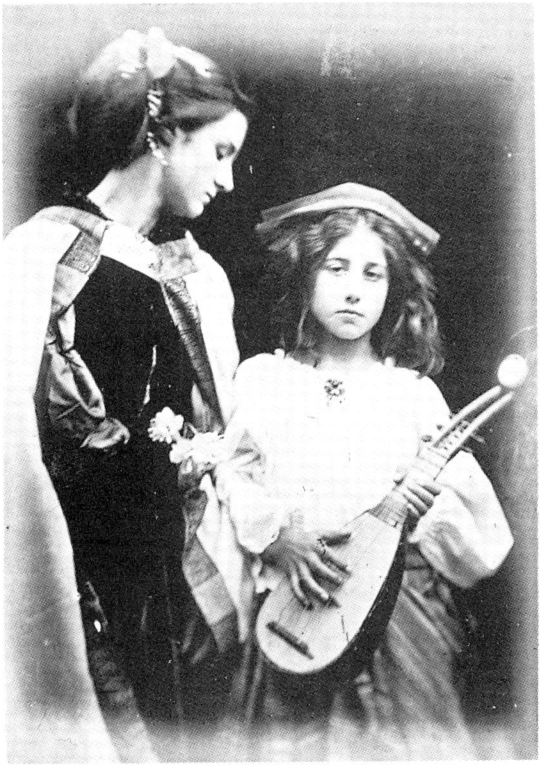

QUEEN ESTHER BEFORE KING AHASUERUS

The models here are Henry Taylor and Mary Ryan, supported by an unknown serving maid.

The Herschel album gives this photograph the title "*King Ahasuerus and Queen Esther in Apocrypha*". This is significant, for the scene depicted comes not from the Old Testament book of *Esther* but from the extra verses which appear in the *Apochrypha*. These derive from the Greek rather than the original Hebrew.

The biblical account tells how the Jewish queen Esther saves her people from a holocaust threatened by the Persian despot Ahasuerus, on the advice of his false minister Haman.

Esther intercedes with the king direct, ignoring great personal danger, and aided by her high priest - and uncle - Mordecai.

Mrs Cameron here chooses a variant on this narrative, drawn from the *Apocrypha*. Esther appears before him in "*glorious apparel*";

"Then lifting up his countenance that shone with majesty, he looked very fiercely upon her, and the queen fell down, and was pale, and fainted, and bowed herself upon the head of the maid that went with her".

This melts Ahaseurus's heart, "*then God changed the spirit of the king into mildness*". One of the end results of such mildness is that " *they hanged Haman on the gallows that he had prepared for Mordecai. Then was the king's wrath pacified*".

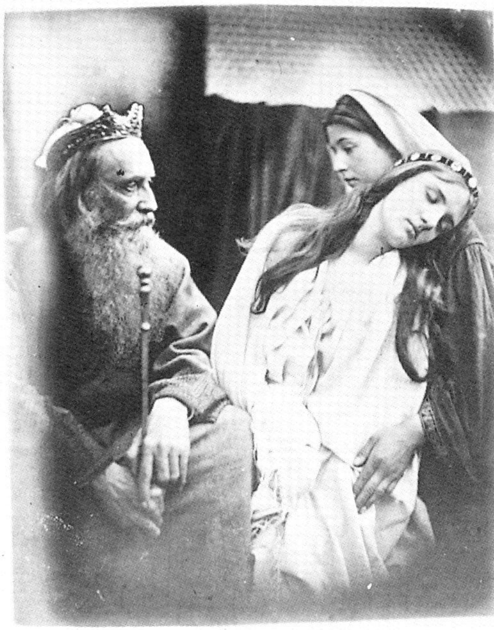

SUMMER DAYS

The models used are May Prinsep, Freddie Gould, Lizzie Keown and Mary Ryan. Freddie Gould often appeared with Mary Hillier in Cameron's religious studies as the infant Christ, or the baby St John.

Another title for this photograph is "*Two Children*". Herschel wrote a letter to Julia - quoted with approval in *Annals of My Glass House* - in which he separates the style of this photograph from the "*high relief*" of "*The Mountain Nymph, Sweet Liberty*".

"The last batch of your photographs is indeed wonderful, and wonderful in two distinct lines of perfection ... "Summer Days" is in the other manner - quite different but very beautiful, and the grouping perfect. "Proserpine" is awful".

Herschel perhaps uses 'awful' in its literal sense of 'awe-inspiring'.

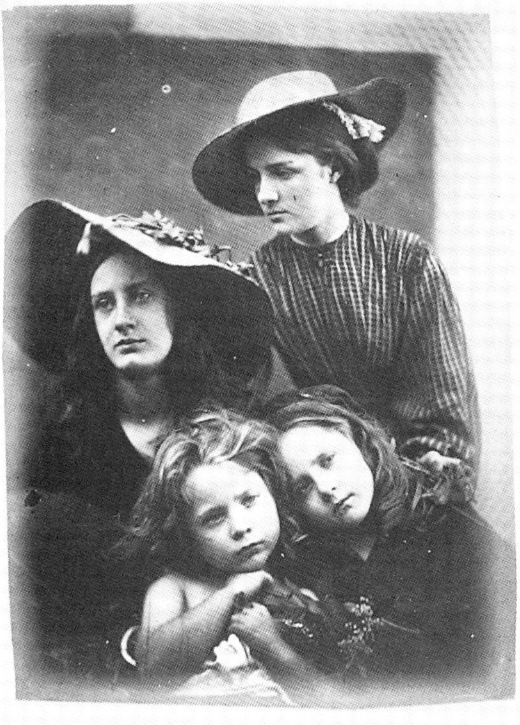

HENRY HERSCHEL HAY CAMERON

Henry Cameron (1852-1911) was Julia's youngest son. Although blind in one eye, he himself was to become a "*Photographic Artist*" with a studio in Cavendish Square, using equipment inherited from his mother. Indeed, photographs by him exist of Julia herself, and of Aubrey Beardsley, who pronounced his own portrait "superb".

As Julia proudly wrote,

"I believe that my youngest boy, Henry Herschel, who is now himself a very remarkable photographer, told me is quite true - that my first successes in my out-of-focus pictures were a fluke. That is to say, that when focussing and coming on something which, to my eye, was very beautiful, I stopped there instead of screwing on the lens to the more definite focus which all other photographers insist on".

Henry, in turn, helped keep his mother's memory alive by publishing *Annals of My Glass House* in 1889. He was doted on by Julia, who chose his bungalow in Ceylon as her final resting place. Henry was also an amateur actor of talent - most memorably as the Carpenter in *Alice in Wonderland*, written of course by his mother's friend and deadly photographic rival, Charles Dodgson.

In a letter to Edward Lear, dated 1873, Emily Tennyson wrote of the strong links; between mother and son.

"It seems so impossible for her to part from this last son who is a comfort to her, and his best hope of work is in Ceylon, though his inclination leads him to try the English stage".

Certainly, Henry often appears in the cast list of the amateur theatricals at "*Mrs Cameron's thatched house*" held in aid of local charities.

Henry Taylor described him, along with his older brother Hardinge, as "*refined and tender as girls*". However, an anonymous relative also relates that he grew up "*given to every sort of vice*"!

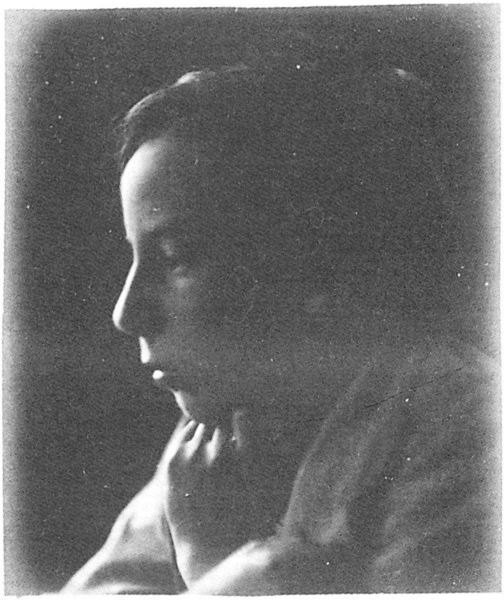

ISABEL SOMERS-COCKS

Isabel was the daughter of Mrs Cameron's youngest sister, Virginia, and Lord Somers - himself an amateur photographer of note.

She and her sister Adeline were over-protected by their mother; by the time she was 18, Isabel had had twenty different governesses, none of whom were able to teach her to spell.

Strictly secluded from other children, Isabel's meals were so carefully regulated by Lady Somers that she often had to buy her sister's breakfast egg!

Again at her mother's bidding, Isabel married Lord Henry Somerset MP. When Isabel discovered that he was conducting a homosexual affair, she exposed him, only to herself be socially ostracised as a result.

Isabel threw herself into good works, becoming president of the British Women's Temperance Association, and set up a farm colony for convicted female drunkards.

In her Journal for February 5th 1872, Lady Tennyson records,

"Mrs Cameron takes up snowdrops & violets gathered by Alfred for Isabel Cock's marriage today".

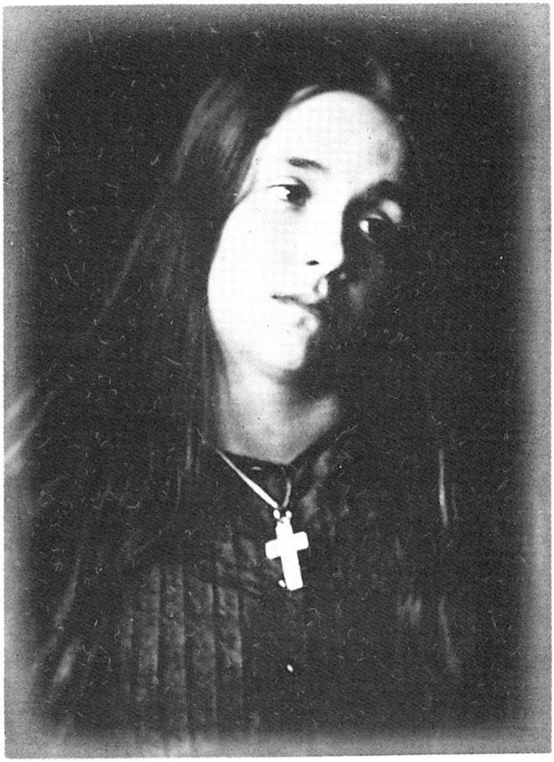

LIONEL TENNYSON

Lionel Tennyson (1854-86) was the poet's second son, born at Farringford. In this photograph he must be in early teens, as he is no longer dressed as a child - the Tennyson children were, like Isabel, over protected and mothered - but in adult clothes slighty too big, to grow into!

William Allingham described Lionel as "*odd, shy, sweet and, as his mother says, daimonisch*". Emily herself records, in a Journal entry for 1866,

"Our Lionel comes looking rosy and happy, thank God, & his stammering nearly cured. He is his father's walking companion ... the boy wonderfully tender & thoughtful, so different from what one often hears of boys!"

Educated at Eton, Lionel later joined the India Office. In 1885 he contracted malaria in Assam, and died on board ship on the voyage back to England. He was buried at sea.

In a poem dedicated to the Governor-General of India, with whom Lionel had stayed during his illness, Tennyson wrote movingly about the untimely loss of his son.

"Not there to bid my boy farewell,
When That within the coffin fell,
Fell - and flashed into the Red Sea,
Beneath a hard Arabian moon
And alien stars".

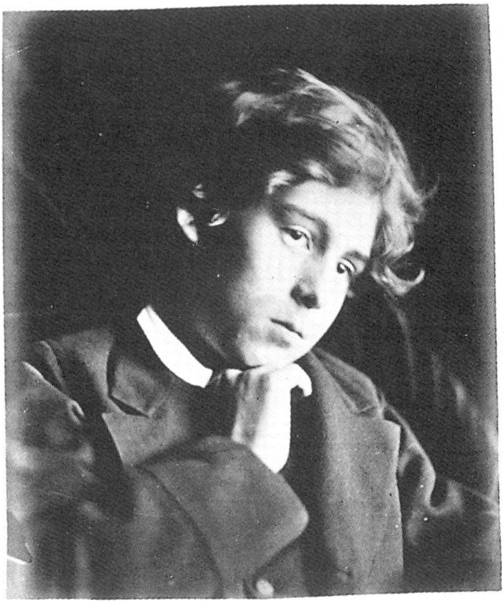

CHARLIE HAY CAMERON:
MY 4TH SON

Named after his father; Charlie was perhaps the son returning from India, in whose honour Mrs Cameron presented a set of her photographs to Brockenhurst station.

Charlie certainly unwittingly delayed his mother's own departure back Ceylon. In a letter to Edward Lear, dated 1873 and sent from Farringford, Emily Tennyson records that

"Poor Mrs Cameron has had a sad time of it lately. Her son Charlie had a dreadful operation to remove part of his jawbone, and this gave such a shock to her nerves weakened by his long previous illness and her persistent disregard of all rules of health for years past that she has been seriously ill".

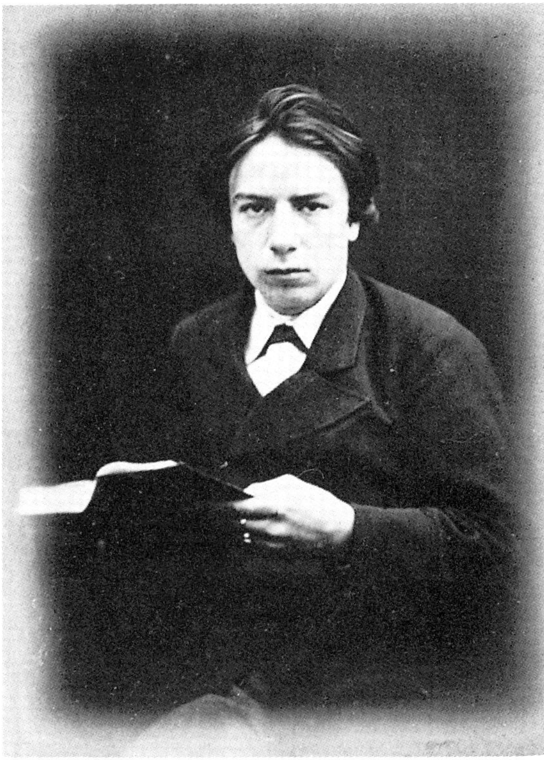

CHARLIE HAY CAMERON

A touching domestic portrait, far less stiff that the more "posed" other portrait.

In *Annals of My Glass House*, Julia records with gratitude the support of her family for her strange hobby,

"Personal sympathy has helped me on very much. My husband from first to last has watched every picture with delight, and it is my daily habit to run to him with every glass upon which a fresh glory is stamped, and to listen to his enthusiastic applause.

This habit of running into the dining room with my wet pictures has stained such an immense quantity of table linen with nitrate of silver, indelible stains, that I should have been banned from any less indulgent household".

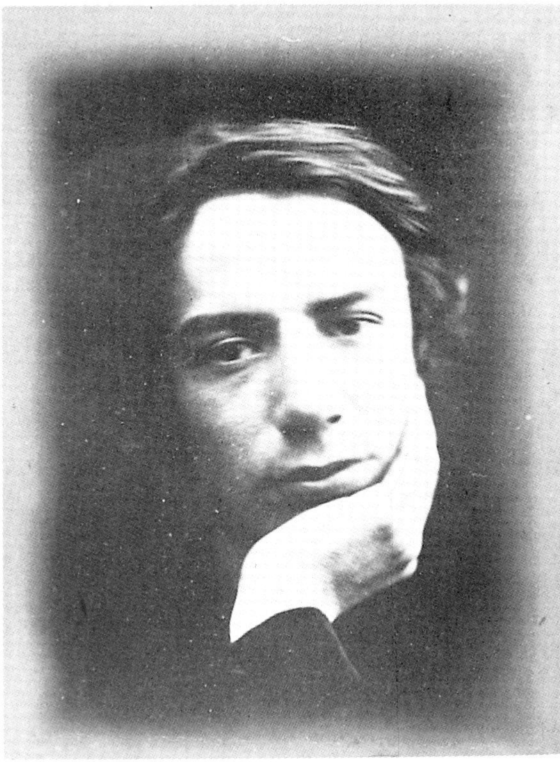

CHRISTABEL: MAY PRINSEP

Christabel is the title of a long poem by Samuel Taylor Coleridge. The first part was written in 1797, in Stowey in Somerset, the second in 1800, at Keswick, after his return from Germany, a poem of erratic metre. The heroine dreams of her lover, a knight far away.

"Each matin bell, the Baron saith,
Knells us back to a world of death".

Coleridge's poem is heavily influenced by German Romanticism, as indeed was Cameron's own translation of Burger's *Leonore.*

This is one of Julia's favourite photographs. In a letter to her, John Herschel wrote of the same portrait,

"Christabel is a little too indistinct to my mind but a fine head".

Another copy of this photograph is sub-titled "*May Prinsep at the age of 14*".

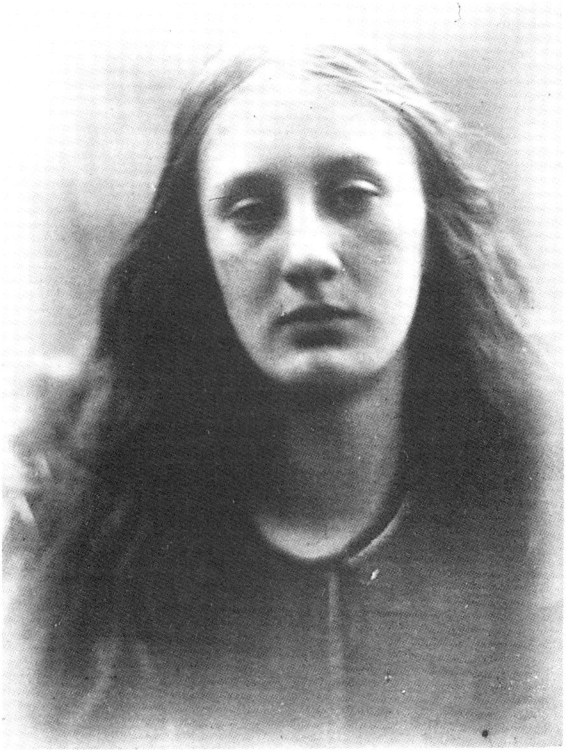

MRS HERBERT DUCKWORTH

In the Herschel album, this is entitled "*Julia J full face*" and subtitled "*My Niece Julia (Julia Jackson)*".

After the death of her first husband, Julia Jackson married Sir Leslie Stephen, editor of the *Dictionary of National Biography*, for which Julia herself wrote the entry on her aunt.

"Mrs Cameron was known and beloved by a large circle of friends. She corresponded with Wordsworth; she was well known to Carlyle, who said, on receiving one of her yearly valentines, "This comes from Mrs Cameron or the devil'. Sir Henry Taylor, a valued friend, says of her ...

'it was indeed impossible that we should not grow fond of her - impossible for us and not less so for the many whom her genial, ardent and generous nature has captured ever since'

... her influence on all classes was marked and admirable. She was unusually outspoken, but her genuine sympathy and goodness of heart saved her from alienating a friend".

In Virginia Woolf's short story *The Searchlight*, Julia Cameron appears "*with clenched fists and threats of damnation*", forcing her subjects to hold still. "*Surely you can put up with a little discomfort in the cause of art*".

Woolf also supplied a short biography of her great aunt, in the Hogarth Press publication *Victorian Photographs of Famous Men and Fair Women.*

A little theatre was built where the young people acted. On fine nights they trapesed (sic) *up to the Tennysons and danced; if it were stormy and Mrs Cameron preferred the storm to the calm, she paced the beach and sent for Tennyson to come and pace by her side.*

The colour of the clothes she wore, the glitter and hospitality of the household she ruled, reminded visitors to the East ... she could be highly despotic. "If you ever fall into temptation", she said to a cousin, "down on your knees and think of Aunt Julia". She was caustic and candid of tongue".

A trait, obviously, inherited both by Julia Jackson and Virginia Woolf herself.

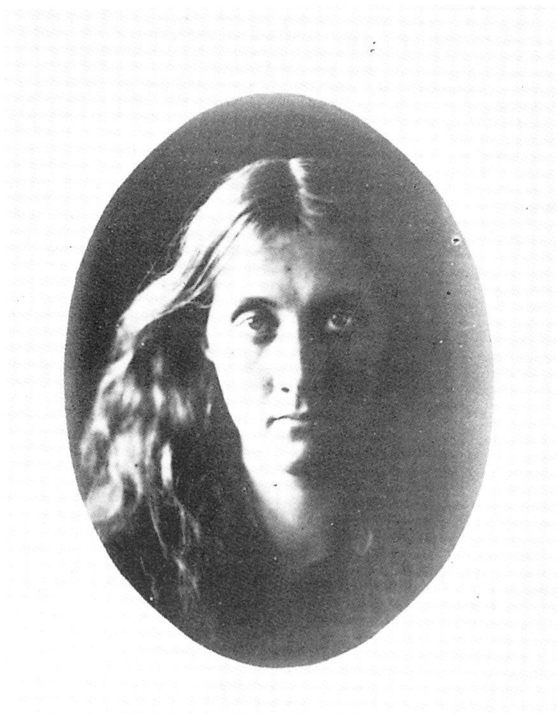

JULIA MARGARET CAMERON FROM A PORTRAIT BY G.F.WATTS 1850 - "LONG LONG AGO"

The original was painted between 1850 and 1852, and presented to the sitter, then still living in East Sheen. It now hangs in the National Portrait Gallery.

Mrs Watts later recorded that

"Two portraits, a painting and a chalk drawing, were made of this remarkable member of the Pattle sisterhood by Mr Watts when as a delicate and fairly young woman she returned from Ceylon.

The grandeur of the vivid being of later years is lacking, whom as yet no written description completely portrays"

Julia bequeathed the painting to her son Hardinge, writing on the back a verse from *The Weeper* by Richard Crashaw, the 17th century English devotional poet.

" Not in the Evening's eyes
When they red with weeping are
For the sun that dyes
Sits sorrow with a face so faire:
No where but here did ever meete
Sweetness so sadd, sadnesse so sweete".

The obituary printed in the *Times* of 4th March 1879 was a good summation of Julia Cameron's life and unquenchable spirit.

"Mrs Cameron's singular ardour of enthusiasm, the energy with which she flung herself into whatever she undertook, her rare forgetfulness of self and readiness to help others, endeared her to a wide circle of friends ...
her devotion to her family was for her a love which nothing ever diminished, not even her departure for a distant island, whither her affection for her children carried her, at a time of life when the long journey and the difficulties and discomforts of forming a new home would to most women have been insurmountable".

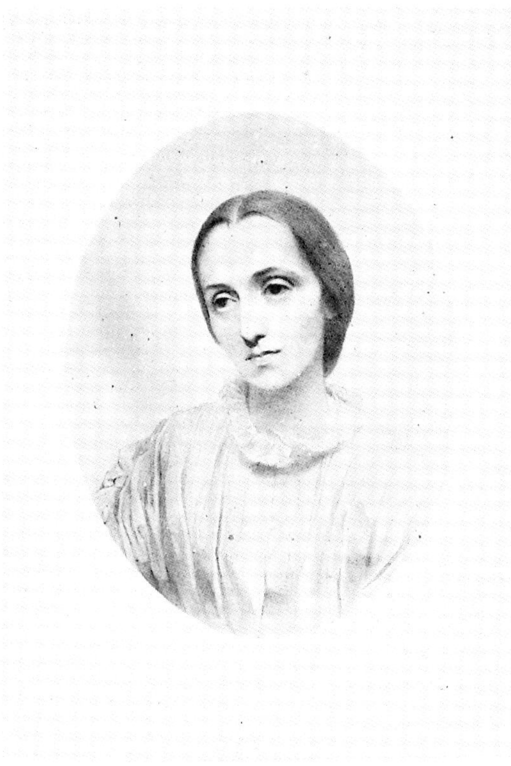

JAMES ROGERS

This photograph is not part of the Nellie Mundy album, but belongs to the Island artist Muriel Owen. James Rogers was her great-great-grandfather. James Henry Thomas Rogers lived at Roseberry Lodge, near Farringford. He was a friend of Tennyson and a naturalist of some distinction. Together with his son, Henry St. John Rogers, he made several journeys to Brazilian jungles to collect specimens of natural history, particularly butterflies. On one of these expeditions Henry was bitten by a snake, the bite eventually proving fatal.

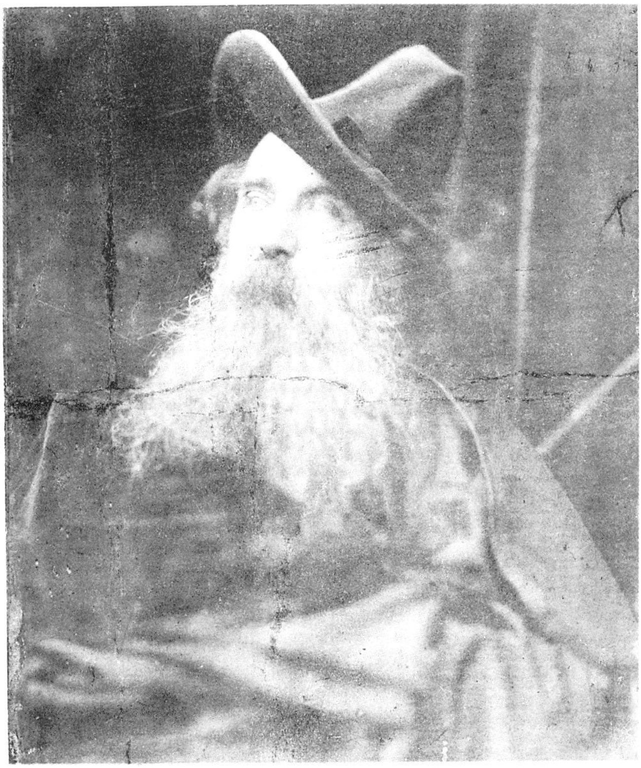

Aftermath

Indeed, Freshwater continued to attract great writers and artists to walk in the footsteps of Mrs Cameron, Watts and Tennyson. Kipling, D.H.Lawrence, George Bernard Shaw, T.S.Eliot - who walked the cliffs, talking of Tennyson - Augustus John, W.H.Auden, Christopher Isherwood, J.B.Priestley and John Betjeman all either lived near or visited the Bay.

Priestley described best the atmosphere of the West Wight, a kind of creative indolence;

"I remember Neville Cardus staying with us on a bright summer week-end, and after a few hours of it saying slowly to me, "It's like a dream".

Just such a sense of intense stillness is caught by Cameron's lens; her photographs are timeless precisely because time is not pressing, because her subjects are in no hurry whatsover, and can therefore examine their own souls.

Julia Margaret Cameron's photographs, once the subject of great amusement, have gradually been accepted as the work of the most influential pioneer of perhaps the most important art form of the 20th century.

The purchase, after a public appeal, of the Herschel album with Colin Ford's subsequent and monumental study; a touring exhibition in 1984 - organised by Southampton University's John Hansard Gallery - which visited Bonn, Paris, Madrid and New York; the enormous retrospective exhibition at Stanford University; the growing number of books on Cameron's life and art: all are signs that Mrs Cameron's full artistic measure is becoming apparent. The purpose of this book is to concentrate attention on Julia's place in a particular community and place, here on the Island.

As Thackeray's grand-daughter was to write:

"To us that live at Freshwater, every stone has significance, every green lane and path association. Great men cast a benediction upon the places where they have lived, and Freshwater is hallowed ground".

It is that rich heritage that we on the Isle of Wight are determined to preserve.